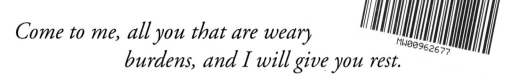

Are you in need of rest? Do you desire the support of others as you further your pursuit of God? Come to the Good Shepherd who will lead you to restful waters and restore your soul.

"I have enjoyed and appreciated the fellowship that this Bible study evoked. The feeling of belonging has helped me feel more a part of my church community. Gwen Meding's work has challenged me to really search the Scriptures. I have been amazed to discover how a certain theme carries through the Gospels and manifests itself in other books of the Bible."

—D. Shain

"I had the privilege of journeying through Advent immersed in these reflections. I follow the Orthodox fast to prepare myself spiritually to receive the blessings of celebrating Jesus, the Light of the world. The structured Scripture readings and insightful and thought-provoking questions enhanced my fasting immeasurably."

—M. Sidic

COME AND REST

SEPTEMBER YEAR A TO JUNE YEAR B

COME AND REST

A BIBLE STUDY FOR ALL
WHO THIRST FOR MORE.

GWEN MEDING

Pleasant Word
A Division of WINEPRESS PUBLISHING

1. Albert Laisnez, *Setting the Stage*, introduction to the first and second readings for Sundays and Solemnities (Edmonton, Kwik Kopy Printing, 1998), used with kind permission.

2. Extract from *The Alpha Course Manual* published by Alpha International, first published 1993. Used by kind permission of Alpha International.

3. *Good News Bible,* introduction to the Deutercanonical/Apocryphal books, Copyright ©1992, American Bible Society. Used by permission.

4. Excerpts from the *New American Bible* with revised New Testament and Psalms, Copyright © 1991, 1986, 1970. Confraternity of Christian Doctrine, Inc., Washington, DC. Used with permission. All rights reserved. No portion of the *New American Bible* may be reprinted without permission in writing from the copyright holder.

5. Taken from the *Handy Bible Dictionary and Concordance* by Zondervan Corporation, Copyright ©1983 by The Zondervan Corporation. Used by permission of The Zondervan Corporation.

6. Excerpts from *Catechism of the Catholic Church,* Copyright © Libreria Editrice Vaticana, 1992. For the English translations in Canada, Copyright @ Conacan Inc., 1994. All rights reserved. Used with permission of the Canadian Conference of Catholic Bishops. (www.cccbpublications.ca)

7. Excerpts from *The New Jerusalem Bible,* copyright © 1985 by Darton, Longman & Todd, Ltd., and Doubleday, a division of Random House, Inc. Reprinted with permission.

8. Brown, Raymond E.; Fitzmeyer, Joseph A.; Murphy, Roland E.; *New Jerome Biblical Commentary,* 1st Edition ©1990. Adapted by permission of Pearson Education, Inc., Upper Saddle River, NJ.

9. Brown, Raymond E.; Fitzmeyer, Joseph A.; Murphy, Roland E.; *Jerome Biblical Commentary, The,* 1st Edition ©1969. Adapted by permission of Pearson Education, Inc., Upper Saddle River, NJ.

10. Scripture quotations are taken from the *New Revised Standard Version* of the Bible, copyright © 1989 by the National Council of the Churches of Christ in the USA. Used by permission. All rights reserved.

ISBN 13: 978-1-4141-1159-9
ISBN 10: 1-4141-1159-2
Library of Congress Catalog Card Number: 2007910284

CONTENTS

SECTION THREE: ORDINARY TIME AFTER CHRISTMAS

SECTION FOUR: LENT

SECTION FIVE: EASTER

APPENDIX ONE

APPENDIX TWO

APPENDIX THREE

ENDNOTES

HOW TO USE THIS BIBLE STUDY

The following ideas are notes and suggestions for this Bible study. I trust you will adapt and personalize the study to fit your group.

This Bible study series follows the Sunday readings in the three-year Catholic lectionary (Year A, B, C). Traditionally a new lectionary year begins with Advent, at the end of November. But our Bible study begins in September; therefore, this study splits the lectionary year to accommodate this. Whatever date in the year your group begins, use the Bible study lesson applicable to the coming Sunday. The *Come* series includes:

Come and Rest—September Year A to June Year B
Come to Me—September Year B to June Year C
Come and Drink—September Year C to June Year A
Come to the Cross—Lenten Study on the Easter Vigil Readings

In the Catholic lectionary, the following dates need to be watched. When Sunday falls on these dates, the feast day readings supersede the Sunday readings:

September 14	Triumph of the Cross supersedes the 24th Sunday.
November 1	All Saints' Day supersedes the 31st Sunday of ordinary time.
November 2	All Souls' Day supersedes the 31st Sunday of ordinary time.
November 9	Dedication of St. John of Lateran supersedes the 32nd Sunday.
February 2	Presentation of the Lord supersedes the 4th Sunday of ordinary time.

Each study is designed to take 2 to 2 ½ hours. If you have a large group, or your group discusses in depth, you may want to do only one of the Sunday readings and use the next cycle for the second reading.

Come and Rest studies the first and second Sunday readings in detail. The gospel is included with the readings to connect the promise in history with its fulfillment in Jesus; and to Jesus' mission as it continues through His church. This background broadens our understanding of the gospel. The second reading is always from the New Testament and takes us through the main parts of the epistles.

1. Study Format: Each week follows the same format. These are suggestions and can be adapted to your group.

- **Opening Song.** A song is helpful to focus on the present moment and leave behind the hectic. Music can create an atmosphere of peace, reflection, and worship. The music you use may be taped or on CD.

- **Opening Prayer.** Have someone open with a brief prayer inviting the Lord into this time and then encourage others to add their prayers. For example, "Lord, may we be aware of Your presence here tonight. We give You permission to work in our hearts. Bless our families. I invite everyone to add your own prayer." Close by reading together the opening prayer that is given in the study.

- **Group Guidelines.** Reviewing these guidelines weekly builds trust and sets boundaries and expectations. All are accepted where they are today and encouraged to grow in faith.

- **Setting the Stage.** This portion is taken, with permission, from Fr. Albert Laisnez's book of the same title. It gives the historical background and setting for the readings. In the original, "parish" and "parishioner" are used. I have changed these to "church" and "Christian" for this series.

- **First Reading.** Read aloud twice. Listen for the word, the phrase, or the idea that stands out to you. Briefly discuss it as a group.

- **Exploring Further.** Through a question format, the reading is broken apart so we can see how corresponding Scriptures and past events are linked. We discover how God's promises in the Old Testament are fulfilled in the New. Over the year we come to see the great scriptural themes woven from Genesis to Revelation. As we hear God's Word, it transforms our minds and hearts. We grow in knowledge and faith. The Scriptures used in this section are mainly taken from the cross-reference Scriptures in *The New Jerusalem Bible*.

- **Reflection.** Take the truths of the Scriptures just discussed and apply them with the help of reflection questions.

- **Optional Exercise.** There is an optional exercise between the first and second readings to give participants a chance to share something about their week. We found this time draws groups closer. As needs are made known, the group has opportunities to help one another. A time limit is needed. Some groups may want to do this exercise at the beginning.

- **Second Reading.** This follows the same format as the first reading.

- **Closing Prayer.** Feel free to do intercessory prayer at the end, add a song, or do whatever the group wants.

2. Using the Bible tips:

- The group may have a variety of Bible translations. This adds richness and understanding and clarifies the meaning. Please note that the numbering of the verses varies in some translations. When there is a discrepancy in numbering, the NRSV translation is the standard used for this study. To clarify when there is a discrepancy, the NRSV verse will be noted and the verse in other translations will be in parentheses. Example: Isaiah 64:8 (or verse 7). The numbering of verses varies in parts of Isaiah, Job, Psalms, Hosea, and the end of Malachi. All Bible quotes, unless otherwise stated, are from the NRSV: *Catholic Edition*, copyright 1993.

How to Use This Bible Study

- When one question has several Scriptures, it helps to have several people look up one verse each.
- Some people may not feel comfortable finding the Scripture references in the "Exploring Further" section. I encourage you to use the index and to assist each other in locating Scriptures. Reassure those who may be intimidated because they are unfamiliar with a Bible. We are all learning.
- When a Scripture verse is long, this study uses a reference letter "a" to indicate the first part and "b" to indicate the second part. For example, Isaiah 43:1 could be divided into Isaiah 43:1a and 43:1b for discussion purposes.

Study Group Guidelines

LISTEN	I will not interrupt, teach, or lecture. I will give everyone an opportunity to speak. I will not chatter or dominate the conversation.
RESPECT	I will allow everyone to share at his or her own comfort level. I will not make judgmental or critical remarks. I will not give unsolicited advice.
CONFIDENTIALITY	I will keep what is said in the group, in the group. I will not share what is not mine to share.
PARTICIPATION	I will participate in the discussion. I will remember that the group is never the same without me. My insights and experiences are valuable to the group.

SECTION ONE
ORDINARY TIME

This Bible study begins in September. This time of the church year is referred to as ordinary time. Ordinary time will continue until the Feast of Christ the King, near the end of November, and it is followed by Advent. Ordinary time or routine time is the best environment for spiritual growth. *This is the time to develop daily practices and habits that build a foundation of faith and a relationship with God.*

The highlight of an athlete's life may be the Olympics or the championship game, but it is the athlete's daily habits and practices that make the highlight possible. The following story, told by Fr. Patrick Martin at a parish mission, illustrates the importance of making good use of ordinary time in our faith life.

A concert pianist told his students to practice so well that if their own strength failed, they would be able to carry on out of habit. Just before a sold-out concert was to begin, the pianist suffered a stroke that left him blind and weak. Those around him wanted to cancel the performance, but he said, "No." With assistance, he was led to the piano. All his years of practice prepared him for this moment. He played flawlessly for his last appearance. Because of the years of daily practice, habit took over when his own strength failed.

A regular routine of our faith practices and prayer habits builds a firm foundation that can be relied on when our own strength fails. *We are building a relationship with God that prepares us for whatever is to come.* The ordinary seasons of our life are important. Use them wisely.

Not that I have already obtained this
or have already reached the goal;
but I press on to make it my
own, because Christ Jesus has
made me his own.

(Philippians 3:12 NRSV)

Twenty-Fourth Sunday of Ordinary Time Year A

Opening Song

Opening Prayer

Open in prayer and invite everyone to add his or her own prayer. Close together: Lord, may we serve You with all our hearts and know Your forgiveness in our lives. Amen.

Review Study Guidelines

First Reading

Sirach 27:30-28:7 (See appendix one)

Setting the Stage

The first reading is from the book of Sirach, also called Ecclesiasticus. This book of wise sayings is written about 180 years before Jesus by a Jew who wants to encourage his fellow Jews to live their faith with love. Through these words, God, our Father, is giving us one of the most difficult challenges of our lives.

Read the first reading aloud. Reread this Scripture. What word, phrase, or idea stands out for you?

Exploring Further

1. What are the two hateful things mentioned in Sirach 27:30 that are part of a sinner's life?

2. If we are vengeful, what will be the result according to Sirach 28:1?

3. What are we called to do in Sirach 28:2?

4. What does Jesus say we are to do?
   Matthew 5:23-24
   Matthew 6:12-15

5. What points are made in Sirach 28:3-5?

6. Describe the mercy that the king showed to the servant in Jesus' story in Sunday's gospel, Matthew 18:23-27.

7. How does the servant who just received mercy treat his fellow servant in Matthew 18:28-31?

8. What is the result of the servant's lack of mercy in Matthew 18:32-34?

9. What is the point of Jesus' story according to Matthew 18:35?

10. If you are finding it hard to forgive someone, what else might you consider?
    Sirach 28:6-7
    Sirach 7:36
    Romans 12:19

Reflection

1. Can you think of a time when you were aware of the mercy and forgiveness of God extended to you? Did this experience make it easier for you to forgive others? Why or why not?

2. Can you think of a situation in the world in which vengeance and unforgiveness have gone on for generation after generation? Why is forgiveness in such difficult circumstances so difficult to grant?

3. Do you consider yourself someone who forgives easily or someone who holds a grudge? Explain.

4. Based on what we've just studied, which Bible verse speaks to you most clearly and convinces you to choose forgiveness?

Optional Exercise: Have each person in the group briefly share about an event from his or her past week or about an upcoming event. This could be a time to share a triumph, trial, or need.

Second Reading

Romans 14: 7-9

Setting the Stage

This short reading is from the letter that St. Paul writes to the church in Rome during the winter of A.D. 57-58. Through these words, God our Father shows us who ought to be the real focus of our lives.

Further Information: This short reading from Romans is taken from a section dealing with conflict over clean and unclean foods. Some Christians in the Roman community were raised under the Mosaic Law, which observes specific dietary laws, and were scrupulous in continuing these practices. This causes a clash with those who believe that under Christ these practices are not necessary because Paul teaches that food is not a source of moral contamination.

Read the second reading aloud. Reread this Scripture. What word, phrase, or idea stands out for you?

Second Reading

Genesis 22:1-2,9-13,15-18

Exploring Further

1. What advice is given in Romans 14:1?

2. What two issues are causing debate in Romans 14:2, 5?

3. How does Paul deal with the conflict and teach what should dictate behaviour where choices differ, and neither choice is sinful, in Romans 14:3-4, 6?

4. What is said regarding God's total claim on the believer in Romans 14:7-9?

5. According to the following Scriptures, what should be our intent?
   1 Corinthians 6:19-20
   2 Corinthians 5:15
   Philippians 1:20

6. Who are we accountable to for how we live and how we treat others?
   Romans 14:10-12
   Matthew 18:32-35

Reflection

1. What conflict exists in your church? Do two or more groups feel strongly about the way something should be done? Paul's instruction was to do everything for God, remember that in life and death all believers belong to God, and do not judge. How could his instruction be applied to your church's situation?

2. What attitudes are we to have in times of conflict? Despite differences, how are we to treat one another?

3. Whether you agree or disagree with changes, what result does obedience have for the whole church?

4. "In essential things, unity; on the questionable points, liberty; in all things, Charity." (Rupertus Meldenius) Can you think of some examples in which diverse practices, cultures, opinions, and perspectives have enriched the entire church locally and/or worldwide?

5. How does continuous arguing and dissent become a distraction from our focus to live for Christ and give Him glory? How does living for Christ translate into choices and actions on a daily basis?

6. How does remembering that we live for Christ and will be accountable to Him keep the importance of our own opinions in perspective?

Closing Prayer

Lord, You are kind and merciful. May Your Holy Spirit influence our thoughts and actions as You guide and direct us. Amen.

TRIUMPH OF THE CROSS
ONLY WHEN SUNDAY FALLS ON SEPTEMBER 14

Opening Song

Opening Prayer

Open in prayer and invite everyone to add his or her own prayer. Close together: We should glory in the cross of our Lord Jesus Christ, for He is our salvation, our life, and our resurrection; through Him we are saved and made free. Amen. (Galatians 6:14)

Review Study Guidelines

First Reading

Numbers 21:4-9

Setting the Stage

The first reading is from the book of Numbers. It describes the escape of the Hebrews from slavery in Egypt in 1300 B.C. They go through the Red Sea and into the Sinai Desert and eventually come to Edom, an area south of the Dead Sea. It is a hot, dry journey and the people complain about "manna," their desert food. The writer is a person of deep faith who interprets all events, both good and bad, as coming from God, including the disaster that follows the complaints. The remedy provided seems very strange. We need to focus on the faith and trust in the hearts of the people as they do what is asked of them. This is an appropriate reading for this feast of the Cross of Jesus, for we too "look with faith and trust" on it, the sign of our healing and peace.

Read the first reading aloud. Reread this Scripture. What word, phrase, or idea stands out for you?

Exploring Further

1. What are the people doing in Numbers 21:4-5?

2. How does God normally provide for them in the desert?
   Exodus 16:11-15
   Exodus 17:2-6
   Deuteronomy 8:15-16

3. What is the consequence of the people's complaining against God and Moses in Numbers 21:4-6?

4. After experiencing the consequence of their complaining, what do the people do and how does Moses respond in Numbers 21:7?

5. What do the following Scriptures tell us about the role of Moses?
   Exodus 32:11-14, 30-32
   Numbers 11:1-2

6. What is the consequence of sin for all people according to Romans 6:23?

7. Who is the mediator that Moses is "a type of" or prefigures in 1 Timothy 2:5?

8. When Moses intercedes, what does God tell him to do (Numbers 21:8-9)? What will happen as a result of Moses' action?

9. What does Jesus compare to the bronze serpent in John 3:14-15? What does He say will happen as a result?

10. How is the bronze serpent misused according to 2 Kings 18:1-4?

11. What truth is remembered in Wisdom 16:5-8?

12. What truth is stated in the following Scriptures?
    Deuteronomy 9:6
    Titus 3:5

13. What is the triumph of the cross according to John 3:16-17?

Reflection

1. The Israelites complain about the water, the food, Moses and Aaron's position of authority, and how powerful the enemy is. How is complaining like a poisonous snake?

2. Do you know someone who shows gratitude, even for small things? What effect do they have on you?

3. The Israelites' complaining against God and Moses is severely punished in today's reading. Another time they start by complaining and then proceed to worship a golden calf and rebel against Moses and his authority. Each time the consequences are severe. Does God punish sins such as complaining, worshiping idols, rebellion, and others as severely today? Why or why not?

4. After being disciplined, the people repent and turn back to God. How has a negative consequence to a choice you have made resulted in a return to God?

5. God heals the Israelites when they look at the bronze serpent, a reminder of their sin. Over time they begin to worship the instrument of healing rather than the healer. When God uses a person, a group, or an object to bless and heal us, what danger is there of lifting up the instrument rather than giving glory to God?

Optional Exercise. Have each person in the group briefly share about an event from his or her past week or about an upcoming event. This could be a time to share a triumph, trial, or need.

Second Reading

Philippians 2:6-11

Setting the Stage
The next reading is from the letter of St. Paul to the church at Philippi, northern Greece. He is writing from a prison perhaps in Western Israel about 30 years after the resurrection of Jesus. The Philippian church sent help to Paul and he writes to thank them and to encourage them in their faith. This reading is actually a quote from an early Christian hymn. Note: "Under the earth" (verse 10) refers to the place of the dead. God our Father through these words is showing us what comes after the cross.

Read the second reading aloud. Reread this Scripture. What word, phrase, or idea stands out for you?

Exploring Further

1. What does Paul beg of the Philippians in Philippians 2:1-2?

2. What should be avoided and what should we try to do according to Philippians 2:3-5?

3. What is Jesus' attitude according to Philippians 2:6-7?

4. What position does Jesus not cling to?
   John 1:1-3
   Hebrews 1:3

5. What does Jesus' becoming human cost him?
    Matthew 20:28
    John 5:17-18
    John 10:31-33
    Romans 8:3

6. To what extent does Jesus humble himself in Philippians 2:8?

7. What is the result of Jesus' action for us according to John 3:14-15, Sunday's gospel?

8. What promise is given to those who humble themselves in Matthew 23:12?

9. How does the cross triumph according to Philippians 2:9-10?

10. What title does the resurrection give Jesus in Philippians 2:11?

11. What possible responses to the death and resurrection of Jesus are suggested in 1 Corinthians 1:23-25?

Reflection

1. Avalanches, volcanoes, tornados, and raging floods are four powerful natural forces. What powerful natural force have you experienced?

2. "The cross of Jesus is the most powerful spiritual force in the universe. This single act has won forgiveness for every sin that has ever been committed, has defeated the devil and his minions that attempt to control our lives, and has ripped the veil that separated heaven from earth and revealed a new and living way to the Father. Have you seen a sin pattern exploded as you turned to the Lord for help? Have you seen a relationship that seemed beyond saving turn around?"[1] Where have you experienced the power of the cross in your life? What situation in your life do you want to take to the cross? What might you be clinging to or grasping for or trying to control in your life that God is asking you to let go of at the cross?

3. The Christian life is full of paradox: dying to receive life, emptying self to be filled, humbling self to be exalted, the first shall be last, deny self and serve others, and many others. Jesus set the example for this way of living, and it often goes against secular culture. How would you describe your desire and motivation to model your life on that of Jesus the Christ? What gives you hope, inspiration, and a hunger to claim and live the victory won for you on the cross?

Closing Prayer

Lord, by Your cross You have redeemed the world. We give You honor, glory, and praise for leading us to life. Amen.

Twenty-Fifth Sunday of Ordinary Time
Year A

Opening Song

Opening Prayer

Open in prayer and invite everyone to add his or her own prayer. Close together: The Lord is near to all who call on Him. Amen. (Psalm 145:18)

Review Study Guidelines

First Reading

Isaiah 55:6-9

Setting the Stage

The first reading is from the book of the prophet Isaiah. These words are spoken to the Hebrew people about 535 B.C. as the first of them are being allowed to return to Palestine after being deported by the Babylonians 50 years earlier. It is a time of discouragement as they struggle to rebuild their lives, their country, and their temple.[2] When our world has collapsed around us, do we, in our thoughts at least, ask the big question, why? How does God respond?

Read the first reading aloud. Reread this Scripture. What word, phrase, or idea stands out for you?

Exploring Further

1. What are we urged to do in Isaiah 55:6?

2. When is a good time to seek God according to 2 Corinthians 6:1-2?

3. What is required of us when we seek God according to Isaiah 55:7a?

4. What action do we need to take according to Isaiah 1:16-17?

5. When we repent and turn to God, how does God respond?
   Isaiah 55:7b
   Psalm 145:18
   Zechariah 1:3
   Luke 15:20

6. When we want God to conform to our ways, plans, wisdom, and knowledge, what should we remember from Isaiah 55:8-9?

7. What do we discover about God's thoughts and ways in Sunday's gospel, Matthew 20:1-14?

8. What is the reaction of the workers to God's generosity in Matthew 20:15?

9. What is the lesson to Jesus' story in Matthew 20:16?

10. Who are the first workers in the vineyard and why might they need to hear this story according to Matthew 19:27-30?

11. What assurance goes with God's ways according to Isaiah 55:10-11?

Reflection

1. In Isaiah 55 we are encouraged to seek God. Are you seeking for God or avoiding Him? Explain.

2. What would be an example of wanting God on our terms rather than on God's terms?

3. In your life, what have you left behind (repented) in order to turn to God? How did you experience God's mercy?

4. What transformation step(s) do we take so our ways and thoughts will be more like God's?

Optional Exercise: Have each person in the group briefly share about an event from his or her past week or about an upcoming event. This could be a time to share a triumph, trial, or need.

Second Reading

Philippians 1:20-24, 27

Setting the Stage

The second reading is from the letter of Paul to the church in Philippi, northern Greece. St. Paul is close to these Christians, so they give him help when he is sent to prison, probably in what is now southwestern Turkey, about 25 years after the resurrection of Jesus. He writes at least a couple of letters that are combined here into one.[3] He wants to thank them and encourage them. Paul's difficulties are not just because he is in prison, but he is also being ridiculed by some Christians.[4] He considers the possibilities—to die or to live? What are the advantages of each? When life seems to put us down, what are we called to do?

Read the second reading aloud. Reread this Scripture. What word, phrase, or idea stands out for you?

Exploring Further

1. What is Paul's desire for his life in Philippians 1:20?

2. What is the goal Paul sets before us?
   Romans 14:8
   2 Corinthians 5:6-9

3. What is our hope in Colossians 3:3-4?

4. What is Paul's dilemma and what are the advantages of each in Philippians 1:21-26?

5. What is Paul's prayer and hope in Philippians 1:27?

Reflection

1. Paul sees dying as an opportunity to be closer to Christ and living as an opportunity to speak boldly for Christ and to serve God's people in order that Christ is glorified. Do you look forward to dying in order to be with Christ? Why or why not?

2. What opportunities do you have in your life to proclaim Christ and serve others day to day?

3. Paul's vision of the church is a people, standing firm in one spirit, striving side by side with one mind for the sake of the gospel. What concrete action can you take to work toward unity in this way?

4. What has to change in you to make such unity possible?

Closing Prayer

Lord, may our footsteps be firm in keeping Your commands that our lives may glorify You. Let our love for You and one another bear good fruit. Amen.

TWENTY-SIXTH SUNDAY OF ORDINARY TIME
YEAR A

Opening Song

Opening Prayer

Open in prayer and invite everyone to add his or her own prayer. Close together: Lord, teach me Your ways that I might walk in them. Amen.

Review Study Guidelines

First Reading

Ezekiel 18: 25-28

Setting the Stage

The first reading is from the book of the prophet Ezekiel. Ezekiel is living during the time the Hebrew people, here called "House of Israel," are conquered by Babylonian armies and many are deported, about 600 years before Jesus was born. The Hebrews are blaming their ancestors for their pain. Through Ezekiel, God our Father speaks of the need for each person to take responsibility for his or her actions.

Read the first reading aloud. Reread this Scripture. What word, phrase, or idea stands out for you?

Exploring Further

1. What do the people accuse God of?
   Ezekiel 18:25a
   Malachi 3:13-15

2. The people think they are being punished for the ways of their ancestors. What does God clarify to them through Ezekiel in Ezekiel 18:4?

3. What does God consider fair according to Ezekiel 18:26-28?

4. How is God and His way described?
   Deuteronomy 32:4
   Psalm 19:7-11

5. How does Jesus explain obedience in Sunday's gospel, Matthew 21:28-31a?

6. Who does Jesus say will enter heaven before the chief priests and elders and why in Matthew 21:31b-32?

7. What does God desire for us according to…?
   Ezekiel 18:21-23
   2 Peter 3:9

8. What does God call us to do in Ezekiel 18:30-32 and what will be the result?

Reflection

1. Have you ever been angry with God and thought He was unfair? Explain.

2. People sometimes say, "If God loves, why does He let innocent people be hurt or bad things happen?" How would you respond to this or a similar statement?

3. Why is it easier to blame God and others than to accept responsibility? Is repentance hard or easy for you? Explain.

4. When we repent and turn from wickedness or selfishness, we receive forgiveness and life. Do you consider this fair? What does this show you about God?

Optional Exercise. Have each person in the group briefly share about an event from his or her past week or about an upcoming event. This could be a time to share a triumph, trial, or need.

Second Reading

Philippians 2:1-11

Setting the Stage

The second reading is from the letter St. Paul writes to the church in Philippi, northern Greece, when he is in a prison, probably in what is now southwestern Turkey, about 25 years after the resurrection of Jesus. Paul knows there are some disagreements among the Christians, so he quotes an early Christian hymn about the Lord Jesus. It is in the second half of the reading. This reading should prompt us to consider what Jesus might do if he were in our shoes as we interact with each other—even, and maybe even especially, when we disagree with each other.

Read the second reading aloud. Reread this Scripture. What word, phrase, or idea stands out for you?

Exploring Further

1. What does Paul beg of the Philippians in Philippians 2:1-2?

2. What should be avoided and what should we do according to Philippians 2:3-5?

3. What does Jesus do according to Philippians 2:6-7?

4. What position does Jesus relinquish?
   John 1:1-3
   Hebrews 1:3

5. What does Jesus' becoming human cost him?
   John 5:18
   John 10:33
   Matthew 20:28
   Romans 8:3

6. According to Philippians 2:8, to what extent does Jesus humble himself?

7. Because of Jesus' being human, what does this obedience cost him according to Matthew 26:36-39?

8. What promise is given to those who humble themselves in Matthew 23:12?

9. How is Jesus exalted according to Philippians 2:9-10?

10. What title does the resurrection give Jesus in Philippians 2:11?

11. What are possible responses to the death and resurrection of Jesus as suggested in 1 Corinthians 1:23-25?

Reflection

1. When has wanting your own way or not getting your own way caused disunity in your family or in a group? Explain.

2. Give an example of someone in a public position who has been humbled because of his or her poor behaviour or choices. How have you experienced being humbled?

3. Give some examples of people who have been honoured by their actions or by the way they lived their lives. What qualities or characteristics did their lives have?

4. God exalts Jesus to the position of Lord. What does this mean to you? Do you see Jesus as your Lord? Explain.

Closing Prayer

<u>A Pledge of Allegiance</u>

I pledge allegiance to Jesus as King and Lord of all.
I promise to put Jesus ahead of any power, person, or thing.
I choose to give Jesus His rightful place as ruler over my life.
I promise to serve Jesus as His faithful and obedient servant,
and to work for the coming of His kingdom.
With the help of His grace, I make this pledge. Amen.

Signed _____

Twenty-Seventh Sunday of Ordinary Time Year A

Opening Song

Opening Prayer

Open in prayer and invite everyone to add his or her own prayer. Close together: Lord, You are the vine and we are the branches. Only as we remain in You can we bear fruit. Apart from You we can do nothing. Amen.

Review Study Guidelines

First Reading

Isaiah 5:1-7

Setting the Stage

The first reading is from the book of the prophet Isaiah. We hear a beautiful poem in which Isaiah speaks first about his people in the southern kingdom of Judah and about their capital city, Jerusalem; and secondly, about the other Hebrew people in the northern kingdom called Israel. He compares them to a vineyard. Notice that Psalm 80 continues this image!

Read the first reading aloud. Reread this Scripture. What word, phrase, or idea stands out for you?

Exploring Further

1. What effort is put into the vineyard according to Isaiah 5:1-2?

2. What does God do for His people, His vineyard, in Psalm 80:8-11?

3. What does God ask the people in Isaiah 5:3-4?

4. What consequence will the vineyard receive for fruitlessness?
Isaiah 5:5-6
Ezekiel 15:6-8

5. Who is the vineyard as explained in Isaiah 5:7a?

6. What does God expect and what does He receive in Isaiah 5:7b?

7. What does Jesus teach in the following Scriptures?
Matthew 7:15-20
John 15:5-8

8. Who is the "true vine" and who is the "vine-grower" according to John 15:1?

9. In Jesus' parable, how does the landowner care for the vineyard and who is entrusted with the vineyard in Sunday's gospel in Matthew 21:33?

10. How do the tenants treat the landowner in Matthew 21:34-39?

11. What punishment do the Pharisees say should befall the tenants in Matthew 21:40-41?

12. What point does Jesus make in Matthew 21:42-46?

Reflection

1. In the above Scriptures God lists what He did for His people. If God gave you a list of what He did for you, what specific things would be on the list?

2. The following reflection is taken from *Secrets of the Vine* by Bruce Wilkinson.

   ➢ If your life consistently bears no fruit, God will intervene to discipline you.
   Discipline is what happens when our loving Father steps in to lift us away from our wrong, destructive, and unfruitful pursuits. "As a man disciplines his son, so the Lord your God disciplines you (Deuteronomy 8:5 NIV). If you have sin in your life—repent!

   ➢ If your life bears some fruit, God will intervene to prune you.
   If disciplining is about sin, pruning is about self. In pruning God asks you to let go of things that keep you from His kingdom purposes and your ultimate good. If God is pruning you, ask God to clearly show you what you need to let go of, and trust Him enough to release it completely to Him.

   ➢ If your life bears a lot of fruit, God will invite you to abide more deeply in Him.
   "I am the vine, you are the branches. He who abides in me bears much fruit" (John 15:5). After discipline to remove sin, after pruning to change priorities—abide in Me. The ancient vineyard reminds me that I can always be "present" with God, no matter what is whirling around me. God invites each of us to be tapped into His purposes and power *all the time*. Brother Lawrence, a seventeenth-century lay Christian who worked

in a monastery kitchen, described his practice of abiding in God: "I do nothing else but abide in His holy presence, and I do this by simple attentiveness and an habitual, loving turning of my eyes on Him. This I call... a wordless and secret conversation between the soul and God which no longer ends."[5]

- Discipline, pruning, and abiding are all necessary in order to produce fruit. To which of these areas can you relate? Explain. Which season of discipline, pruning, or abiding are you currently in now? Why do you think so?

3. What kind of fruit do you think God expects from His people? What kind of fruit do you see in your Bible study group, in the local church, and in the universal church?

Optional Exercise. Have each person in the group briefly share about an event from his or her past week or about an upcoming event. This could be a time to share a triumph, trial, or need.

Second Reading

Philippians 4:6-9

Setting the Stage

The second reading is from St. Paul's letter to the church in Philippi, northern Greece. The Christians there have become dear to him and it is striking that he can write these words from a prison cell! The time is about 25 years after the resurrection of Jesus. Through St. Paul, God our Father is giving us clear guidelines on how we can find peace in our lives.

Read the second reading aloud. Reread this Scripture. What word, phrase, or idea stands out for you?

Exploring Further

1. What does Paul say to do in Philippians 4:4? Why is it more impressive considering that Paul is writing from prison?

2. What does Paul say not to do in Philippians 4:6a?

3. What does Jesus say about worry or anxiety in Matthew 6:25-34?

4. Instead of worry, what are we to do and with what attitude in Philippians 4:6b?

5. What will be the result according to Philippians 4:7?

6. What does Jesus promise in John 14:27?

7. What should we fill our thoughts with according to Philippians 4:8?

8. What does Paul encourage believers to keep doing in Philippians 4:9?

9. What wisdom is expressed in the following Scriptures?
   Hebrews 6:11-12
   Hebrews 13:7
   Titus 2:7-8

10. When we imitate people of faith, whose example are we following?
    Matthew 16:24
    John 13:15
    1 Peter 2:21-23

Reflection

1. Both Jesus and Paul say "do not worry." Do you think worrying and anxiousness are a choice? Why or why not? On a scale of 1 to 10, what is your worry or anxiety level today?

2. Can we worry and trust with gratitude at the same time? Why or why not?

3. We are encouraged to fill our mind with whatever is true, noble, right, pure, lovely, admirable, excellent, and praiseworthy. How might we do this on a daily basis? How would trauma, crisis, and pain affect how you might apply this Scripture in your life; for example, during a war, a tornado, chronic illness, or torture?

4. Why do you think faithful Christian role models are necessary? What results when Christ's followers poorly model the Christian life? What leaders and lay people in our time have been good role models to imitate?

Closing Prayer

Take a few minutes and identify your worries and anxieties. Have each person present these concerns to God. Then the group can help pray, petition God, rejoice, and give thanks. Expect God's gift of peace.

Twenty-Eighth Sunday of Ordinary Time Year A

Opening Song

Opening Prayer

Open in prayer and invite everyone to add his or her own prayer. Close together: If You, O Lord, should mark iniquities, Lord, who could stand? But there is forgiveness with You, so that You may be revered. Amen. (Psalm 130:3-4)

Review Study Guidelines

First Reading

Isaiah 25:6-10a

Setting the Stage
The first reading is from a special part of the book of the prophet Isaiah called the "Apocalypse of Isaiah." We hear of a vision of heaven—a promise of what God our Father has in store for us. Note the phrase "on this mountain." This refers to Mount Zion, the hill on which Jerusalem is built; it becomes a symbol of heaven, it also has become a symbol of us, the church. Can we see how these words apply to this very celebration?

Read the first reading aloud. Reread this Scripture. What word, phrase, or idea stands out for you?

Exploring Further

1. What will the Lord provide for His people and where according to Isaiah 25:6?

2. What heavenly food does Jesus provide according to John 6:51, 54?

3. Who will be gathered to the Holy Mountain?
   Isaiah 25:4
   Isaiah 56:6-8

4. How did those invited to the banquet respond in Sunday's gospel, Matthew 22:1-8?

5. When the first guest did not come, who was invited?
   Matthew 22:9-10
   Luke 14:21-23

6. Who will be thrown out according to Matthew 22:11-14?

7. How do we put on a "wedding robe"?
   Matthew 3:8
   Matthew 7:21
   Ephesians 4:22-24
   Revelation 19:7-8

8. Who does Jesus say to invite to a banquet and why in Luke 14:12-14?

9. What will God accomplish "on this mountain," the heavenly Jerusalem?
   Isaiah 25:7-8
   Isaiah 35:9-10
   1 Corinthians 15:26
   Revelation 21:4

10. What will the people who turned to God declare according to Isaiah 25:9-10a?

Reflection

1. God is preparing a feast on His holy mountain. All have been invited to share in the messianic banquet but not all accept the invitation. What do you think might be reasons why people do not accept this invitation? What actions would indicate an affirmative response to the invitation?

2. What excuses do you use when Jesus invites you to the mini-banquet of daily prayer?

3. We put on wedding clothes by producing fruits in keeping with repentance, obedience to the will of the Father, putting off our old self, renewing our mind and putting on our new self like God in righteousness and holiness, and by righteous acts. What choices and actions will assure we are clothed in "wedding robes"? How are such actions a result of God's mercy rather than our own efforts? And how does that change the way some people feel about their attempts to earn an invitation to the wedding feast?

4. Who do you invite to your home? Who is not invited and why?

5. In Isaiah 25:7-8, God promises to remove the veil, defeat death, wipe away tears, and remove disgrace. Which of these promises is most meaningful to you today? Explain.

Optional Exercise. Have each person in the group briefly share about an event from his or her past week or about an upcoming event. This could be a time to share a triumph, trial, or need.

Second Reading

Philippians 4:10-14, 19-20

Setting the Stage

The second reading is from the letter of Paul to the church in Philippi, northern Greece. St. Paul is very close to these Christians, so they help him when he is sent to prison, probably in what is now southwestern Turkey, about 25 years after the resurrection of Jesus. He writes at least two letters that are combined here into one. St. Paul never takes a salary, but he does accept the assistance they give him, and he is writing to thank them. He also states clearly who he always relies on. Who can we always rely on?

Read the second reading aloud. Reread this Scripture. What word, phrase, or idea stands out for you?

Exploring Further

1. What gives Paul joy?
   Philippians 4:10
   Philippians 1:3-5

2. What has Paul learned and what does he recommend?
   Philippians 4:11-12
   Hebrews 13:5
   2 Corinthians 12:9-10

3. How is Paul able to live this way according to Philippians 4:13?

4. Why is Paul eager to accept the Philippians' gift according to Philippians 4:17?

5. What further clarity is given to Paul's meaning of "crediting to your account" in 1 Timothy 6:17-19?

6. How does Paul describe the Philippians' gift in Philippians 4:18?

7. What does the analogy of a "fragrant offering" refer to in the following Scriptures?
   Genesis 8:20-22
   Ephesians 5:1-2
   Hebrews 13:15-16

8. How does Paul say God will provide for the Philippians in Philippians 4:19?

9. What is God's promise regarding giving (tithing) in Malachi 3:10?

Reflection

1. How have you experienced joy working with others in a good work, project, or ministry?

2. What are you dissatisfied with? How might you learn be content in this situation?

3. How might someone living in poverty understand God's promise to "supply every need according to his riches in glory in Jesus Christ"? How has God provided for you in a difficult time?

4. What do you have in abundance that you can share? What does your community/country have in abundance and how might it share?

Closing Prayer

Lord, of ourselves we can do nothing. We rely on You for all we have and for all we are. Help us to be generous in sharing what we have with others. Amen.

Twenty-Ninth Sunday of Ordinary Time Year A

Mission Sunday

Opening Song

Opening Prayer

Open in prayer and invite everyone to add his or her own prayer. Close together: Lord, guard us as the pupil of Your eye and hide us in the shadow of Your wing. Give us joy, strength, and trust as we serve You. Amen.

Review Study Guidelines

First Reading

Isaiah 45:1, 4-6

Setting the Stage

The first reading is from the book of the prophet Isaiah. These words are spoken about 540 years before Jesus. The Hebrew people have been conquered and deported by the Babylonians about 50 years earlier. And the Babylonians are in turn conquered by the Persians in 539 B.C. The Persians' foreign policy is very different; instead of deportation, they see that peace could be better maintained by supporting local customs. Thus, they allow the Hebrew people to return to their country and they even help them in the work of reconstruction. Note the names "Jacob" and "Israel," which refer to the entire Hebrew people. Note also that the king of Persia at the time is a man called Cyrus, and Cyrus is not a believer in God. Yet listen to how he is described! Does God our Father make "unreligious" persons and events the instruments of good for us?

Read the first reading aloud. Reread this Scripture. What word, phrase, or idea stands out for you?

Exploring Further

1. What title, reserved for kings of Israel, is this foreign "pagan" king given, and what is his mission according to Isaiah 45:1-2?

2. What mission is Jesus anointed to do in Luke 4:18-21?

3. What does God do for Cyrus and why according to Isaiah 45:4?

4. What do the following Scriptures say about being called by name and being chosen?
   Isaiah 43:1
   John 10:3
   John 15:16
   Ephesians 1:4-5

5. Why did God give King Cyrus victory and bless him according to Isaiah 45:3-6?

6. What truth is emphasized in Isaiah 45:5a?

7. What do the following Scriptures say about God?
   Isaiah 44:6-8
   Amos 4:13

8. How do the Pharisees treat our anointed King, Jesus, in Sunday's gospel, Matthew 22:15?

9. What is the trap laid for Jesus in Matthew 22:16-17?

10. What does Jesus' response teach us about obedience to God and obedience to earthly authority in Matthew 22:15-21?

11. What result does Jesus' answer have on those trying to trap him in Matthew 22:16?

Reflection

1. Just as God used the pagan king, Cyrus, God can use any person or situation as His agent. What person or situation did God use as an agent to work in your life?

2. God chose Cyrus for the mission of helping to restore Israel. The church is called to carry on the mission of Jesus. According to Vatican II, the mission of the church is to:

   I. Evangelize—meaning to tell the whole world the good news of Jesus Christ;
   II. Sanctify—meaning to help everyone enter in to the Good News, be empowered, made holy, and have mature lives that give life; and
   III. Renew the face of the earth—meaning to establish right relationship of the temporal order, society and all things.[6]

- There are many hard, unjust, and sad situations in our world. How might God work in and through these situations to bring about His purpose and plans? How do you take part in the mission of the church to evangelize, sanctify, and renew the face of the earth?
- Do you believe God has called you by name and chosen you to share in His mission (now the mission of the church) and make a difference in the world? Why or why not?

3. Just as God chose King Cyrus, he chooses leaders today. With this in mind, what does "Give to Caesar what is Caesar's, and to God what is God's" mean to you?

Optional Exercise. Have each person in the group briefly share about an event from his or her past week or about an upcoming event. This could be a time to share a triumph, trial, or need.

Second Reading

1 Thessalonians 1:1-5

Setting the Stage

The next reading is from a special part of the Bible—the first of all the writings of the New Testament. It is the first letter St. Paul writes, only about 20 years after the resurrection of Jesus, to the church in Thessalonica, northern Greece. Paul is writing to encourage the new Christians who have become dear to him when he and his coworkers, Silvanus and Timothy, set up their church a year earlier in the midst of persecution. As you listen to this passage, change the phrase "church of the Thessalonians" to your own church's name. God our Father is speaking to us here just as He did to the Thessalonians through Paul.

Read the second reading aloud. Reread this Scripture. What word, phrase, or idea stands out for you?

Exploring Further

1. Who are Paul's two companions that helped in establishing the church and who now send greetings in 1 Thessalonians 1:1?

2. What three principle Christian virtues are at work in this community according to 1 Thessalonians 1:2-3?

3. How are these three virtues to be used according to 1 Thessalonians 5:8?

4. What do we discover regarding these virtues in 1 Corinthians 13:13?

5. What does Paul remind the Thessalonians of in 1 Thessalonians 1:4?

6. What impacts the lives of the Thessalonians and what gives them power according to 1 Thessalonians 1:5?

7. What does Paul say about his preaching and the Holy Spirit in 1 Corinthians 2:4-5?

8. What demonstrates that the gospel is not just an intellectual exercise for the Thessalonians, but changed their lives in 1 Thessalonians 1:6?

9. If we only give intellectual assent to the gospel, what happens when trials come according to Matthew 13:20-21?

Reflection

1. The three main Christian virtues are faith, hope, and love. Where do you see these virtues at work in your local church and/or the universal church?

2. In your life, how have you experienced the difference between giving intellectual assent to the gospel and having the gospel impact and change your life?

3. The Thessalonians became imitators of Paul, Silas, and Timothy in spite of severe suffering. They welcomed the message with joy as a result of the Holy Spirit. What effect has trials and suffering had on your faith? Who has been a faith example you could imitate, especially in suffering times?

4. "The gospel is more than a proclamation, it is the whole new economy of salvation."[7] Since the gospel of Jesus Christ brings salvation, what does this call you to do through word and action?

5. When your Christian lifestyle attracts someone's attention and that person asks why you live the way you do, what will you tell him or her and what invitation would you extend to that person?

Closing Prayer

Lord, empower us to shine on the world like bright stars, offering it the Word of Life. Amen.

THIRTIETH SUNDAY OF ORDINARY TIME
YEAR A

Opening Song

Opening Prayer

Open in prayer and invite everyone to add his or her own prayer. Close together: Lord, may we remember Your goodness to us and thus give generously to all in need. Amen.

Review Study Guidelines

First Reading

Exodus 22:21-27

Setting the Stage
The first reading is from the book of the exodus. This part of the book is called "the Book of the Covenant." Moses applies the Ten Commandments to daily living. Through these words, God our Father speaks about the need to love the poor and the marginalized of society. Note the reference to the time that the Hebrew people are slaves in Egypt, which is from about 1700 to 1300 B.C.

Read the first reading aloud. Reread this Scripture. What word, phrase, or idea stands out for you?

Exploring Further

1. What are the people to remember in Exodus 22:20?

2. Who are the Israelites instructed not to mistreat and why in Exodus 22:21?

3. What does God hear and what will be the response according to Exodus 22:22-24?

4. How are the poor to be treated according to Exodus 22:25-27?

5. How are we to act according to Isaiah 1:17?

6. In today's reading, Moses is teaching the people a right attitude toward God and those who are less fortunate. What is the attitude and motive for asking Jesus a question in Matthew 22:34-36?

7. How does Jesus sum up the attitude we are to have toward God and others in Sunday's gospel, Matthew 22:37-40?

Reflection

1. The Israelites are often encouraged to remember when they were slaves in Egypt. We too should remember where we have come from in life's journey. Below are some typical life happenings. In the ones that apply to you, what do you remember from your experience and what was helpful to you at that time?

   a. When you moved to a new community
   b. During struggles in your marriage
   c. During struggles in your religious vocation
   d. When your children were small and/or teenagers
   e. During bereavement
   f. Some other crisis

2. We are encouraged to treat the foreigner, widow, and orphan with justice. Who are the vulnerable in our society who need justice or protection? Where is our generosity needed today?

3. We are to lend money to the needy without interest. How might this wisdom be applied by rich countries of the world lending to the poor countries of the world? What have been the results when interest is charged by first world countries to third world countries?

4. The teacher of the law asked Jesus a question to test him, not to learn. How can we approach Scripture, church teaching, and life with a teachable heart? What difference can our motives for wanting answers make to our faith journey?

Optional Exercise. Have each person in the group briefly share about an event from his or her past week or about an upcoming event. This could be a time to share a triumph, trial, or need.

Second Reading

1 Thessalonians 1:5-10

Setting the Stage

The next reading is from the first letter St. Paul writes to the church of Thessalonica, which is located in the northern province of Greece called Macedonia. He is writing from Corinth, located in the southern province called Achaia. Paul and his new converts are facing persecution from unbelieving Jews in Thessalonica, and he writes to praise the new Christians for their faith and perseverance. Can we see ourselves being addressed by God our Father in this reading?

Read the second reading aloud. Reread this Scripture. What word, phrase, or idea stands out for you?

Exploring Further

1. How did the gospel come to the Thessalonians according to 1 Thessalonians 1:5?

2. In spite of harsh persecution, how do they respond in 1 Thessalonians 1:6?

3. What can happen to faith when trials come, and what does this say about the faith of the Thessalonians according to Jesus' parable in Matthew 13:20-21, 23?

4. What fruit of the Holy Spirit is manifest in this church in 1 Thessalonians 1:6b?

5. What other fruits of the Spirit are mentioned in Galatians 5:22-23?

6. What is the result of their faith according to 1 Thessalonians 1:8-9?

7. What is mentioned in 1 Thessalonians 1:9b that others are especially impressed with?

8. What are the Thessalonians steadfastly waiting for according to 1 Thessalonians 1:10?

Reflection

1. Have you experienced the preaching of the gospel in such a way that you could use the expressions "impacted with power" or "causing conviction"?

2. In the midst of persecution, the Thessalonian church manifested joy. What person or group do you know that manifests joy in their faith walk? Who has impressed you by how they lived their faith and what effect did their witness have on your life?

3. People are impressed that the Thessalonians turned from idols. "The gentiles must return to God by forsaking idols, the Jews must turn to the Lord by acknowledging Jesus as Lord."[8] In your culture today, what would be considered a radical change from the norm that would be an impressive witness?

Closing Prayer

Lord, open our hearts to the power of Your Word so we can stand firm in faith until You return. Amen.

THIRTY-FIRST SUNDAY OF ORDINARY TIME
YEAR A

Opening Song

Opening Prayer

Open in prayer and invite everyone to add his or her own prayer. Close together: Lord, we desire to honor You in our hearts and serve You with integrity. May we be faithful to all You call us to do. Amen.

Review Study Guidelines

First Reading

Malachi 1:14-2:2, 8-10

Setting the Stage

The first reading is from the book of the prophet Malachi. "Malachi" is not a name; it is the Hebrew word for "my messenger." We know only a little about the messenger who writes this part of the Bible. He lives about 500 years before Jesus and he shows himself to be a patriotic Jew who knows and loves his Jewish faith. We hear harsh words to priests who do their work poorly or without sincerity.

Read the first reading aloud. Reread this Scripture. What word, phrase, or idea stands out for you?

Exploring Further

1. What insights regarding "the covenant of Levi" are found in the following Scriptures?
   Numbers 18:1-3, 6-7
   Deuteronomy 18:1-8

2. In what way does it appear that the priest and temple assistants from the line of Levi are displeasing God?
   Malachi 1:11-14
   Malachi 2:7-9

3. What admonition is given to the priests in Malachi 2:1-2, 9a?

4. What does Jesus tell the people to do in Sunday's gospel, Matthew 23:1-3?

5. What does Jesus criticize the Pharisees and teachers for in Matthew 23:4-7?

6. For all people who profess to worship God, seek God, or teach the things of God, what is clearly God's way?
   Matthew 23:11-12
   John 13:13-15
   James 1:22
   Isaiah 1:14-17

7. What relationship does God's people have with one another according to Malachi 2:10?

8. How do the Israelites break faith according to Malachi 2:11-12?

9. Why is intermarriage forbidden according to Deuteronomy 7:1-4?

10. What does Paul say about Christians marrying unbelievers in 2 Corinthians 6:14-18?

Reflection

1. The priests displeased God by seeing sacrifice as a burden, by offering diseased and injured animals, by withholding the best offering, by not honouring God in their hearts, by failing to preserve knowledge and give instruction, causing others to stumble, and by doing pious acts to draw attention to themselves. How can we avoid seeing sacrifice as a burden and not giving our best? When leaders do not preserve knowledge or give instruction, how does this affect those they are responsible to teach? How can it cause others to stumble?

2. Good leaders and role models are humble, they serve others, they not only listen to the Word but do as it says, they repent, they seek justice, they encourage the oppressed, they defend the orphan and widow, and they preserve knowledge and give instruction. How have you benefited from sound knowledge and instruction? Do you know someone who is a good role model and servant leader? How can you grow in humility, service, obedience, and helping the less fortunate?

3. Jesus told the people to do what the leaders teach, not as they do. Can you relate to saying the right thing but not doing it? Explain. Why is it important to do what is right, even if those in authority do not?

4. God told the Israelites not to marry foreigners or they would begin to worship other gods. Paul warns believers not to marry unbelievers. Is this still valid advice today? Why or why not? How does the situation differ when someone comes to believe and is already married? What challenges do marriages of different faiths or belief systems face?

Optional Exercise. Have each person in the group briefly share about an event from his or her past week or about an upcoming event. This could be a time to share a triumph, trial, or need

---

Second Reading

1 Thessalonians 2:7-9, 13

Setting the Stage

This letter is from the first letter St. Paul writes to his dear friends—the Christians in Thessalonica, northern Greece, 21 years after the resurrection of Jesus. St. Paul is a tentmaker by trade and wants to support himself rather than rely on offerings from his people. This is to prove to them and others that he is not out for their money.

Read the second reading aloud. Reread this Scripture. What word, phrase, or idea stands out for you?

Exploring Further

1. What words and images are used to relate caring and relationship in 1 Thessalonians 2:7, 11-12?

2. How does Paul exhibit genuine love while witnessing in 1 Thessalonians 2:8-10?

3. Besides proclaiming the gospel, what do the apostles do so they are not a burden in 1 Thessalonians 2:9?

4. What is Paul grateful for according to 1 Thessalonians 2:13?

5. For the gospel to bring conversion, what must happen first?
    Ephesians 1:13a
    Romans 10:17

6. Then what must the message penetrate?
    Romans 10:8-10

7. Then how must the message be received?
    1 Thessalonians 1:6
    Mark 4:20

A brief summary of the Apostolic Tradition, the gospel message is first "received" or "heard." It then penetrates the mind or heart, where if it is welcomed it proves that the hearer acknowledges that God has been speaking through His missionary.[9]

8. Paul rejoices that the Thessalonians received the Word of God. What do the following Scriptures and quotes reveal about God's Word?
    Psalm 119:105
    Isaiah 55:10-11
    John 1:1, 14
    John 17:17
    Hebrews 4:12-13
    James 1:21

    - "All Sacred Scripture is but one book, and that one book is Christ, because all divine Scripture speaks of Christ, and all divine Scripture is fulfilled in Christ."[10]
    - "Ignorance of Scripture is ignorance of Christ." (St. Jerome)

Reflection

A mature Christian says to a young, enthusiastic believer, "You love to witness to people, don't you?" "Yes, I do," is the hasty reply. "But do you love the people you witness to?" he probed. He knew the possibility of witnessing to people without necessarily loving them.[11]

1. What is the difference between loving to witness and loving the people you witness to?

2. Paul is gentle among the Thessalonians, like a mother caring for her little children. He loves them and is delighted to share the gospel and his life because the people are so dear him. He deals with them as a father—encouraging, comforting, and urging them to live lives worthy of God. What can we learn from Paul's example about how to impart the gospel?

3. The gospel message must be heard, must penetrate your heart and mind, and be welcomed into your heart and life. What might the result be if one of these steps is missing? Did all three steps occur in your life? What missionary did God use to speak His gospel through to reach you?

4. The Word of God is a lamp to guide us, accomplishing God's purpose. It literally is God and it became flesh in Christ. It is truth—living, active, and a sword that penetrates thoughts and attitudes. And ultimately it saves us. How have you experienced God's Word in your life?

5. What Scripture verse is meaningful, helpful, encouraging, or a favourite for you?

Closing Prayer

God of power and mercy, only with Your help can we offer You fitting service and praise. May we live the faith we profess and trust Your promise of eternal life. Amen.

All Saints' Day
Only When Sunday falls on November 1

Opening Song

Opening Prayer

Open in prayer and invite everyone to add his or her own prayer. Close together: Lord, we give to You praise and glory and wisdom, thanksgiving and honour and power and strength to our God forever and ever. Amen.

Review Study Guidelines

First Reading

Revelation 7:2-4, 9-14

Setting the Stage

The first reading is from the book of Revelation. It is written by a Christian named John about A.D. 100 and is meant to encourage Christians to persevere in their faith as they face persecution and trials. It is an inspired picture book appealing to our imagination. The pictures are not to be interpreted literally; they are intended to create a total impression of eternal realities. The book of Revelation is an "epic of Christian hope," the victory song of the church. The symbols in this reading are:

1. The number 144,000: this is a multiple of 12; "12" in the Bible is a symbol of completeness. "144,000" means the immense crowd of all those who have been faithful; not one is missing in heaven.
2. A "seal [or mark] on the forehead": like a badge, a seal is a symbol of belonging to God.
3. Palm branches: a palm branch is a symbol of victory.
4. "The Elders": angels in heaven, and symbols of the 12 patriarchs and 12 apostles.

5. "The Four Living Creatures": four angels directing the universe.
   We hear the answer to the question: Will wrongs ever be righted?

Read the first reading aloud. Reread this Scripture. What word, phrase, or idea stands out for you?

Exploring Further

1. Where are the angels stationed in Revelation 7:1?

2. Why is this significant?
   Jeremiah 49:36
   Ezekiel 7:2-4

3. What do the elect receive before disaster comes in Revelation 7:2-3?

4. What sign or seal is given in the following and why?
   Exodus 12:7, 12-14
   Ezekiel 9:3-6
   2 Corinthians 1:21-22
   Ephesians 1:7, 13

5. Who receives the seal and what does this number mean according to "Setting the Stage" and Revelation 7:4?

6. How does this fulfill the promise made to Abraham in Genesis 15:5?

7. Where are these people from? What is everyone doing? What do the palm branches symbolize? What does John see according to Revelation 7:9-12?

8. Who are these people according to the following verses?
   Revelation 7:13-15
   Revelation 15:2-3
   Daniel 12:1-3

9. How are the saints purified according to Revelation 7:14?

10. What does the blood of Christ do?
    John 6:53-56
    Romans 5:9

11. What is the reward to the faithful according to Revelation 7:16-17?

12. What does Jesus promise to the faithful in Sunday's gospel, Matthew 5:1-12?

Reflection

1. Those who receive the seal are faithful, wise, and righteous; grieve and lament detestable things done; hear the gospel and receive it. "Entry to the kingdom by means of a firm decision expressed in action."[12] The gift of salvation is a free gift, paid for by the blood of Jesus that we cannot buy or earn, only receive. Upon receiving this gift we are the property of Jesus and now live a surrendered life of our heart, mind, and soul to his kingship. How would you explain this paradox of free gift, requiring our all?

2. Jesus said those who live vulnerable lives trusting God, who are humble, who hunger and thirst for righteousness, are merciful, pure of heart, peacemakers, and who stand firm when persecuted for righteousness will be rewarded. Are you willing to surrender every area of your life so God can transform you into the type of person described in the beatitudes, regardless of the cost? Explain.

3. On All Saints' Day we remember the communion of saints, those who have been faithful and now enjoy the reward of God eternally sheltering, caring for, and comforting them. What "saint" is an example and encouragement to you?

Optional Exercise. Have each person in the group briefly share about an event from his or her past week or about an upcoming event. This could be a time to share a triumph, trial, or need.

Second Reading

1 John 3:1-3

Setting the Stage

The next reading is from the first letter of John. It is written around A.D. 90 to the Christians who are close to St. John the Apostle. The problem is they are divided over their beliefs. On this feast of All Saints' Day, we hear God our Father tells us *who* we are as human beings, and *what* we, with the saints, can expect after this life.

Read the second reading aloud. Reread this Scripture. What word, phrase, or idea stands out for you?

Exploring Further

1. According to the following, how has God shown his love for us?
   1 John 3:1
   John 3:16
   Romans 8:37-39

2. Who can become God's children according to John 1:12?

3. How will the world treat God's children and why? (See appendix two)
   John 15:20-21
   John 16:2-3

4. We are God's children now. What will we become?
   1 John 3:2
   Philippians 3:20-21
   Colossians 3:4
   1 Corinthians 13:12

5. If we value His promise, how will we act?
   1 John 3:3
   Hebrews 12:1-2
   Matthew 5:48-6:6

Reflection

1. Today on All Saints' Day we celebrate God's children who received Jesus, believed in His name and stood firm to the end. Can you think of how some of these saints were received and treated in this world? How are you treated in this world because of your faith?

2. The following is a description of what God's children will become according to the Scriptures we read today. We do not know what our bodies will be like, we will be like Him, we will be citizen's in heaven, our bodies will be transformed to be as His glorious body, we will appear with Him in glory, we see poorly now as in a mirror and then we will see face-to-face and know fully and be fully known. What does this description suggest to you? Does it give you hope? Why or why not?

3. Until Jesus comes again, we are called to purify ourselves, pray, and do good works, not for show but for God. What are practical ways we can seek to live this way?

Closing Prayer

Lord, we thank You for the saints and their witness to us. Since we are surrounded by so great a cloud of witnesses, let us also lay aside every weight and the sin that clings so closely, and let us run with perseverance the race that is set before us, looking to Jesus the pioneer and perfecter of our faith (Hebrews 12:1-2). Amen.

All Souls' Day
Year A
Only When Sunday Falls On November 2

Opening Song

Opening Prayer

Open in prayer and invite everyone to add his or her own prayer. Close together: We thank You that the favors of the Lord are not exhausted and Your mercies never end. They are renewed each morning, so great is Your faithfulness. Amen.

Review Study Guidelines

First Reading

Lamentations 3:17-26

Setting the Stage

The first reading is from the book of Lamentations, which is written by a Jew following the destruction of Jerusalem by Babylonian armies in 587 BC. The writer describes in a powerful way the grief of the Jewish people and gives us words to express our mourning over the death of loved ones. God our Father through these words tells us what He wants us to do in our grieving.

Note: The liturgical context of these readings on All Souls' Day is that of praying for the dead who are not yet in heaven. All who have died in God's grace and friendship, but still imperfectly purified, are indeed assured of their eternal salvation, but after death they undergo purification, so as to achieve the holiness necessary to enter the joy of heaven.[13]

Instead of assuming those who have died are already in heaven, the church prays for them.

Read the first reading aloud. Reread this Scripture. What word, phrase, or idea stands out for you?

Exploring Further

1. Babylonian armies have destroyed Jerusalem. How does the prophet describe his grief and the grief of the Jewish people in Lamentations 3:16-20?

2. What does the prophet choose to do in the midst of his grief in Lamentations 3:21-24?

3. What truths about God are proclaimed in the following Scriptures?
   Exodus 34:6-7
   Psalm 73:26
   Isaiah 30:18

4. What advice is given in the following Scriptures?
   Lamentations 3:25-26
   Psalm 40:1-2

5. What does the prophet say is good to do in Lamentations 3:27-28?

6. What promise does Jesus give in Matthew 11:28-30, Sunday's gospel?

7. To bear the yoke: do God's will.[14] What is the cost and reward of doing God's will in John 12:23-26, the alternative Sunday gospel?

Reflection

1. The prophet describes his affliction and mourning as being deprived of peace, having forgotten happiness, the future is lost, the present events are bitter, and the events replay over and over. How have you experienced situations in your life that brought about similar thoughts? Is it comforting for you to hear such powerful emotions described in Scripture? Why or why not?

2. In the midst of pain the prophet declares truth. Some statements of truth we read today are: the favors of the Lord are not exhausted, His mercies are not spent, great is His faithfulness, the Lord is good to the one who waits for Him and seeks Him, it is good to wait in silence, the Lord is compassionate and gracious, the Lord hears our cry, He gives us rest when we come to Him. Today we remember those who have died. How might these Scriptures be helpful in your times of grief?

3. How have you chosen to declare the truths of Scripture in the midst of a trying circumstance? What was the result? What might be an obstacle to following this prophet's example of declaring truth in the midst of trial and pain?

Optional Exercise. Have each person in the group briefly share about an event from his or her past week or about an upcoming event. This could be a time to share a triumph, trial, or need.

Second Reading

1 Corinthians 15:51-57

Setting the Stage

The next reading is from the first letter St. Paul writes, about A.D. 55, to the church in Corinth, Greece. Many Greeks at this time think the human body has no value after death. Earlier in this letter, God our Father speaks about the body of Jesus being part of His resurrection. We ask, "But how?" And He answers through these words of St. Paul.

Read the second reading aloud. Reread this Scripture. What word, phrase, or idea stands out for you?

Exploring Further

1. What mystery does Paul reveal in 1 Corinthians 15:51?

2. Why must we change according to 1 Corinthians 15:50?

3. How will we change?
   1 Corinthians 15:52-53
   Philippians 3:20-21

4. When will this change take place according to 1 Corinthians 15:52a?

5. What is the function of the trumpet according to Numbers 10:2-3, 9-10?

6. What trumpet call is yet to come and what will happen when it is blown?
   Matthew 24:30-31
   1 Thessalonians 4:16

7. When we are clothed with the imperishable, what will be defeated according to 1 Corinthians 15:54-57?

8. While we wait, what attitude and way of living is called for?
   1 Corinthians 15:58
   2 Corinthians 5:1-10

Reflection

1. When you consider your own eventual death, what in these readings is the most comforting to you?

2. Whose death was hardest for you to experience? What helped you through it?

3. Pope John Paul II called choices contrary to God and life the "culture of death." In the face of death and the pressure of the culture of death choices, what causes you to persist on your Christian journey?

Closing Prayer

Lord, You have the victory over death, and Your mercy is great. Bring all those who have died into the joy of heaven. Amen.

Dedication of St. John Lateran
Only when Sunday falls on November 9

Opening Song

Opening Prayer

Open in prayer and invite everyone to add his or her own prayer. Close together: Lord we desire that from our heart flows streams of living water out to a thirsty people. Amen.

Review Study Guidelines

First Reading

Ezekiel 47:1-2, 8-9, 12

Setting the Stage

The first reading is from the book of the prophet Ezekiel. These words are inspired by Ezekiel and written by his followers as the Jewish community struggles to keep their Jewish faith while in exile in Babylon (modern-day Iraq) in the sixth century B.C. Note the name "Arabah": it is the name of the dry valley south of the Dead Sea. This is an appropriate reading as we celebrate the dedication of a special church, a special "temple," called the Cathedral Church of the Popes. We hear of a vision showing the importance of God our Father's presence in the temple in Jerusalem, and what good effects would flow from Him to His people who are faithful.

Read the first reading aloud. Reread this Scripture. What word, phrase, or idea stands out for you?

Exploring Further

1. What is Ezekiel shown in Ezekiel 47:1-2?

2. The sea of salt water referred to in Ezekiel 47:8 is the Dead Sea where nothing can live, yet what is promised in Ezekiel 47:9?

3. What results from the water flowing from the temple according to Ezekiel 47:7-8, 12?

4. What effect does water have in the following Scriptures?
   Ezekiel 19:10
   Jeremiah 17:7-8
   Zechariah 13:1

5. What connection does this river of life flowing from the temple have to the river in Genesis 2:8-10?

6. How is the river in Ezekiel similar to the river mentioned in Revelation 22:1-3 and what does the river in Revelation symbolize?

7. How does Jesus refer to Himself in Sunday's gospel, John 2:18-22?

8. What flows from this temple in John 19:34?

9. On the last day of the Feast of Tabernacles, what does Jesus stand up and proclaim in John 7:37-38? (Note: *heart* could be translated as "innermost being.")

   On the Feast of Tabernacles, thousands of Jews go to Jerusalem to celebrate the feast in remembrance of the time Moses brought water from a rock. They thank God for providing water in the past year and pray that He would do the same in the coming year. They look forward to a time when water will pour out of the temple, as prophesied by Ezekiel, becoming deeper and deeper and bringing life, fruitfulness, and healing wherever it flows. This passage in Ezekiel 47 is read at the Feast of Tabernacles and enacted visually. The high priest goes down to the pool of Siloam and fills a golden pitcher with water. He then leads the people to the temple, where he pours water through a funnel in the west side of the altar, and into the ground, in anticipation of the great river that will flow from the temple. According to Rabbinic tradition, Jerusalem is the navel of the earth and the temple of Mount Zion is the center of the navel (its "belly" or "innermost being").[15]

10. What is the result to those who believe in Jesus?
    John 7:38
    John 4:13-14

11. What prophesy concerning the temple does Jesus make and what is He referring to in Sunday's gospel, John 2:18-22?

12. How are the people of God described in 1 Corinthians 3:16-17?

    This is amazing. Ezekiel prophesies that water will flow from the temple and bring life. Jesus says He is the temple that provides living water. All who believe are the temple of God. Living water flows from the temple (believers in Jesus) fulfilling the prophesy in Ezekiel!

Reflection

1. The water flowing from Jesus (His Spirit) brings life, healing, and abundance so much so that places of death can be transformed into places of life. Are you parched and thirsty, sipping occasionally, wading cautiously, or immersing yourself in the living water? Explain.

2. Where and when has this life of Jesus, flowing through the church and/or believers (the community) nourished you or brought life or healing?

3. The living water of Jesus flows through the heart of the believer. The CCC (2563) says, "The heart is the dwelling-place where I am, where I live; the heart is our hidden centre. The heart is the place of decision, the place of truth, where we choose life or death. It is the place of encounter; it is the place of covenant." What image or understanding does this give you? What does this say about the extent and depth of a living relationship with Jesus?

4. St. Teresa of Avila reflects on the interior journey and how there is little or no spiritual growth without growth in self-knowledge. Can you identify examples of where you have grown in self-knowledge as you have matured on your spiritual walk?

Optional Exercise. Have each person in the group briefly share about an event from his or her past week or about an upcoming event. This could be a time to share a triumph, trial, or need.

Second Reading

1 Corinthians 3:9-11, 16-17

Setting the Stage
The next reading is from the first letter St. Paul writes to the church in Corinth, Greece, about 25 years after the resurrection of Jesus. He has received reports that there are divisions in the Corinthian church over the question about which of their priests they will follow. In response Paul compares a church to a building. Through these words God our Father tells us who the foundation of the church is—the One who keeps everyone together. These are appropriate words as we celebrate the famous building called St. John Lateran.

Read the second reading aloud. Reread this Scripture. What word, phrase, or idea stands out for you?

Exploring Further

1. What does Paul compare the Corinthians (and us) to in 1 Corinthians 3:9?

2. How does Paul describe his work and how does he build it in 1 Corinthians 3:10-11?

3. How are believers described?
   Ephesians 2:19-22
   1 Peter 2:4-5

4. What does Paul want clearly understood and what makes the Christian community a fit abode for God in 1 Corinthians 3:16?

5. What does Paul say to preachers and teachers who destroy rather than build in 1 Corinthians 3:17?

6. How does Paul describe the spiritual work of leaders and teachers in the church, and who will judge their work according to 1 Corinthians 3:10b-15?

7. What happens in the temple and how does Jesus react in Sunday's gospel, John 2:13-17?

8. What do the following Scriptures say about the temple?
   2 Corinthians 6:16
   Revelation 21:22

Reflection

1. The church is both visible and spiritual. We need visible reminders of invisible truths. St. John Lateran is a visible church that reminds us that Jesus entrusted the visible church to be the keeper of the faith and to speak and pass on truth in His name. What does this say about the important teaching role of the church? What responsibility does this give teachers and leaders in building and cultivating the lives of each generation?

2. What might happen when we think of the temple or church in terms of a building or institution only? Do you see the people of God being the dwelling place or temple and/or the church being the body of Christ and the spotless spouse? Explain. How do these images change or expand your understanding of church?

3. When you consider yourself a living stone in the temple of the living God, what does this say to you regarding your value? What does it say to you about the value of those you worship with each week?

Closing Prayer

Lord, we desire to be like living stones built on Christ as a spiritual house, a holy people. Amen.

THIRTY-SECOND SUNDAY OF ORDINARY TIME YEAR A

Opening Song

Opening Prayer

Open in prayer and invite everyone to add their his or her prayer. Close together: Lord, help us seek wisdom each day so we will be a light for You now and prepared when Christ comes again. Amen.

Review Study Guidelines

First Reading

Wisdom 6:12-16 (See appendix one)

Setting the Stage

This reading is from the book of Wisdom, written only about 50 years before Jesus. It is meant to encourage Jews who live in the midst of an unbelieving society in Alexandria, Egypt. We hear about God our Father's wisdom; it is described as if it were a separate person, in fact, as if it were a beautiful woman.

Read the first reading aloud. Reread this Scripture. What word, phrase, or idea stands out for you?

Exploring Further

1. How is wisdom described in Wisdom 6:12a?

2. How do we discover Wisdom?
   Wisdom 6:12b
   Proverbs 8:17
   Jeremiah 29:12-13
   Matthew 6:33
   Matthew 7:7-9

3. What are some practical ways we might seek Wisdom?
   Wisdom 6:13-15, 17-18
   Psalm 119: 14-16
   Sirach 6:18-20, 23-26, 34-37 (See appendix one)
   Luke 5:16

4. How is wisdom revealed to us according to 1 Corinthians 1:24?

5. What do these Scriptures say about Wisdom seeking us?
   Wisdom 6:16
   Proverbs 8:1-4
   Isaiah 65:1-2
   John 15:16
   Romans 5:8

6. What response does Wisdom call us to make?
   Deuteronomy 11:1
   Sirach 2:15 (See appendix one)
   Matthew 13:44-46

7. What makes the bridesmaids foolish in the parable in Sunday's gospel, Matthew 25:1-3?

8. How do the wise bridesmaids prepare in Matthew 25:4?

9. What life circumstances happen to all the bridesmaids in Matthew 25:5-8?

10. Where do the foolish bridesmaids go to purchase oil and what results in Matthew 25:9-12?

11. What summary to the parable and words of wisdom does Jesus give in Matthew 25:13?

Reflection

1. What people in your life have been a model and teacher of wisdom? What effect have these people had on your journey? Why is it important to have role models and mentors in your life?

2. To seek and respond to wisdom, according to the above Scriptures, we are encouraged to delight, study, and meditate on God's Word; be disciplined in prayer and study; heed advice; learn from wise persons; spend time alone in prayer; obey God's teaching; and give up whatever we must to obtain the kingdom

(wisdom). How can you implement or increase one or more of these actions in your life? To stay awake is to be open to the Holy Spirit. What can help us stay awake or be open to the Holy Spirit?

3. Where or how did Wisdom find you?

4. In Sunday's gospel, the bridesmaids are all people waiting for Christ. The oil is the wisdom and grace of the Holy Spirit we accumulate as we seek and respond to wisdom throughout life. Why is the "oil" of the Holy Spirit not transferable to those who neglect the things of God? What causes you to lose track of what is important and to neglect the things of God? Why is it foolish to try and buy the things of God in the worldly marketplace?

Optional Exercise. Have each person in the group briefly share about an event from his or her past week or about an upcoming event. This could be a time to share a triumph, trial, or need.

Second Reading

1 Thessalonians 4:13-18

Setting the Stage

This reading is from the first letter St. Paul writes to the Christians in Thessalonica, Greece, in A.D. 51. In this church there is a great expectation that the second coming of Jesus, His return to earth in glory, will take place any day. But what about their friends who have already died? What happens to them? In answer to these questions, Paul gives an impressive poetic description of the second coming; picture a medieval king's dramatic entrance into his castle.

Read the second reading aloud. Reread this Scripture. What word, phrase, or idea stands out for you?

Exploring Further

1. What are we to be aware of according to 1 Thessalonians 4:13-14?

2. What reason for hope is there for the Thessalonians and for us?
   John 14:1-4
   Romans 6:8
   1 Corinthians 15:1-5, 22
   1 Corinthians 15:51-52

3. What will happen according to 1 Thessalonians 4:16-17?

4. While waiting for Christ, what are we to do according to 1 Thessalonians 4:18?

Reflection

1. What images of the second coming do these readings create in your mind? When reading and reflecting on the second coming of Jesus, are you encouraged and hopeful or anxious? Explain.

2. All who have fallen asleep in Christ will rise with Christ. How has this truth given you comfort? Is it wise and compassionate to share this truth with someone, or would it be preachy and insensitive? Explain.

Closing Prayer

Lord, help us to be watchful and ready, for we do not know when the Son of Man is coming. Amen.

Thirty-Third Sunday of Ordinary Time Year A

Opening Song

Opening Prayer

Open in prayer and invite everyone to add his or her own prayer. Close together: Lord, our joy is in serving You and walking in Your ways. Grant us wisdom to use wisely the gifts and talents You give us. We are grateful for all our many blessings. Amen.

Review Study Guidelines

First Reading

Proverbs 31:10-13, 16-18, 20, 26, 28-31

Setting the Stage

The first reading is from the book of Proverbs. This book of wise sayings is put together over a very long period, reaching its final form about 500 years before Jesus. We hear God our Father extolling the virtues of a beautiful woman, an ideal housewife who uses her talents and wisdom to serve others. Because the book is 2,500 years old, obviously the kinds of household activities of those days are very different from household duties of people today.

Read the first reading aloud. Reread this Scripture. What word, phrase, or idea stands out for you?

Exploring Further

1. What attributes of the woman are specified in Proverbs 31:10-12?

2. How is Wisdom described in Proverbs 3:13-18?

3. How does the woman make use of her time and talents in Proverbs 31:13, 16-18?

4. How do the servants use their talents and responsibility in Sunday's gospel?
   Matthew 25:14-16
   Matthew 25:17
   Matthew 25:18

5. How is each servant rewarded?
   Matthew 25:19-21
   Matthew 25:22-23
   Matthew 25:24-28

6. As servants of Jesus, we must give an account of how we administer the gifts in our charge. What is the result of using the gifts given to us so the kingdom on earth may grow, as expressed in Sunday's gospel, Matthew 25:29-30?

7. In the following Scriptures what is of value?
   Proverbs 31:10, 30
   Proverbs 12:4
   1 Peter 3:3-4

8. What does this woman do in Proverbs 31:20, 26?

9. What attitude toward the poor does God expect of us?
   Deuteronomy 15:7-11
   Proverbs 14:31
   Proverbs 21:13
   Matthew 25:34-46

10. What is the woman's reward for living with integrity in Proverbs 31:28-29?

Reflection

1. In what way do you give of your expertise, resources, and time to the poor and needy?

2. Who are the women you admire and for what qualities?

3. What gifts have you been given to help build the kingdom on earth with? How can we exercise our gifts with integrity?

Optional Exercise. Have each person in the group briefly share about an event from his or her past week or about an upcoming event. This could be a time to share a triumph, trial, or need.

Second Reading

1 Thessalonians 5:1-6

Setting the Stage

The next reading is from the first letter St. Paul writes to the church in Thessalonica, Greece, 21 years after the resurrection of Jesus. The burning question of the day is: When will Jesus come back again? God our Father is telling us how we are to prepare for the coming of Jesus.

Read the second reading aloud. Reread this Scripture. What word, phrase, or idea stands out for you?

Exploring Further

1. How will Jesus come according to 1 Thessalonians 5:1-3?

2. What does Jesus say regarding His return in Sunday's gospel, Matthew 24:36, 42?

3. What imagery is used in 1 Thessalonians 5:4-5?

4. What does it mean to be "in the light" or "in the dark"?
   Ephesians 5:8-9
   John 8:12

5. How are we to prepare according to 1 Thessalonians 5:6?

6. What do these Scriptures say about how to prepare and the need to prepare?
   Luke 21:34-36
   Romans 13:10-14
   1 Thessalonians 5:8, 11, 14-18
   1 Peter 1:13-16
   1 Peter 4:7-11

7. What hope does 1 Thessalonians 5:24 give?

Reflection

A young student rushes into the library where a wise pastor is working. "Sir," he says, "what would you do if you knew Jesus were to come back in ten minutes?" The wise man calmly puts down his pen, giving the young man his undivided attention. "Why," he says, "I would continue writing this letter so the Master will find me faithfully carrying out my duties."

1. What duties are you responsible for right now? If Jesus came back today, would He find you faithfully fulfilling these duties?

2. We are exhorted to live our lives so as to be awake, alert, and ready for the second coming of Jesus. What in your life causes you to become sleepy, inattentive, or distracted? In what ways are you prepared for the second coming? In what ways are you unprepared?

3. What helps you stay alert, awake, and attentive to God's priorities in your life?

Closing Prayer

May the God of peace Himself make you perfectly holy and may your spirit, soul, and body be preserved blameless for the coming of our Lord Jesus Christ. The one who calls you is faithful, and He will also accomplish it.

CHRIST THE KING SUNDAY
YEAR A

Opening Song

Opening Prayer

Open in prayer and invite everyone to add his or her own prayer. Close together: Lord Jesus, we acknowledge You as our King. May we find joy and fulfillment in service to You. Amen.

Review Study Guidelines

First Reading

Ezekiel 34:11-12, 15-17

Setting the Stage

The first reading is from the book of the prophet Ezekiel. Ezekiel lives about 600 years before Jesus at the time when the Hebrew people are conquered and deported by the armies of Babylon. God our Father speaks these consoling words to His people. Christ the King Sunday marks the end of the church year.

Read the first reading aloud. Reread this Scripture. What word, phrase, or idea stands out for you?

Exploring Further

1. Who will tend God's sheep according to Ezekiel 34:11-12?

2. What will the Lord do for His sheep according to Ezekiel 34:16?

3. From the following Scriptures what do we discover about Christ as Shepherd?
   Psalm 23:1-4
   Isaiah 40:11
   Matthew 18:12-14
   John 10:11-15

4. What do these Scriptures say about Christ's role as King?
   Ezekiel 34:17
   Matthew 25:31-34, Sunday's gospel

Reflection

1. What type of sheep do you see yourself as: lost, strayed, injured, weak, fat, strong, afraid, hungry, or other? What has Jesus rescued you from?

2. In the above Scriptures Jesus the Good Shepherd heals, strengthens, brings justice, nourishes, quenches our thirst, restores our souls, leads us, carries us, seeks us out when we are lost, protects, and lays down His life for us. At this time in your life, what do you need to receive from your Shepherd and King? How has Jesus cared for you?

3. Jesus seeks out the lost. Do you trust Jesus to care for your loved ones who are lost, strayed, or injured? Explain.

Optional Exercise. Have each person in the group briefly share about an event from his or her past week or about an upcoming event. This could be a time to share a triumph, trial, or need.

Second Reading

1 Corinthians 15:20-26, 28

Setting the Stage
This reading is from the first letter St. Paul writes to the church in Corinth, Greece, about 25 years after the resurrection of Jesus. Many Greeks have questions about life after death. In answer, Paul compares Jesus with Adam. What a different impact each of their lives has on us! Through St. Paul's words, God our Father is telling us what is in store for those who follow His Son, Christ the King.

Read the second reading aloud. Reread this Scripture. What word, phrase, or idea stands out for you?

Exploring Further

1. How does death enter the world and who brings life in 1 Corinthians 15:21-22?

2. What do the following Scriptures make clear regarding sin and *all* people?
   Romans 3:23-24
   Romans 5:18-19
   Romans 6:23

3. Who will be raised from the dead according to 1 Corinthians 15:23?

4. What will take place after the resurrection of the dead?
   1 Corinthians 15:24
   Matthew 25:31-33, Sunday's gospel

5. What reward is given to those who act with compassion in Matthew 25:34?

6. What are the criteria for judgement according to Sunday's gospel, Matthew 25:35-40?

7. What punishment is given and why in Sunday's gospel, Matthew 25:41-46?

8. What hope for resurrection do we have?
   John 11:25
   Romans 8:10-11
   Colossians 2:13-14

9. What do the following Scriptures say about the sovereignty of Jesus?
   1 Corinthians 15:24-2
   Philippians 2:9-11
   Colossians 1:16
   Revelation 19:11-16

10. What will be the last enemy destroyed according to 1 Corinthians 15:26?

Reflection

1. What would you like written on your gravestone? What would you want to hear Jesus say when you arrive in heaven?

2. Compassion and mercy are acted on when we feed the hungry, give refreshment to the thirsty, welcome the stranger, clothe the naked, and visit those who are sick or in prison. Are you engaged in some of these activities?

3. The last enemy to be destroyed will be death. How have you encountered spiritual realities at the time of someone's death?

4. Picture Jesus returning in majesty and awesome power. Do you look forward to this time with joy, anticipation, hope, fear, anxiety, confusion, avoidance, or other? Why?

Closing Prayer

Jesus, You are the Lamb who was slain and is worthy to receive strength and divinity, wisdom and power and honor. You are Lord and King of all and will reign forever and give Your people peace. Bring us to the joy of Your kingdom. Amen.

SECTION TWO
ADVENT/CHRISTMAS

The word Advent means "to come."

The first Sunday of Advent begins the new church year. The four Sundays of Advent are a time to prepare and wait in joyful hope.

We prepare and wait to celebrate when Jesus, the Son of God, came as a human being.

We celebrate Jesus, the Son of God, present in our midst sharing his ministry with us.

We prepare and wait in joyful hope for when Jesus, the Son of God, returns in glory. Are we ready to greet him?

Other Advent words are: Be Alert, Be Ready, and Be Awake!

Advent is a time to ask questions like…
- In what condition is the stable of my heart?
- Do I say, "No room here," or do I make room?
- Am I willing to say yes to God, allowing Jesus to be born in my heart and willing to present Him to the world?
- Am I ready to greet Jesus the King when He returns in glory?

Maranatha! Come, Lord Jesus!

Christmas

Advent ushers in the Christmas season when we celebrate God coming to His people as a baby—the Word made flesh, Jesus.

There are three parts to Christmas:
1. The Christmas experience, when God comes to us.
2. The Epiphany moment, when we recognize the truth of our Messiah and follow the light. We fall to our knees in adoration.
3. Baptism, which includes repentance, being renewed by the Spirit, and sent forth to live and proclaim the good news of Jesus.

The result of this threefold Christmas experience is conversion—a daily event of saying yes to our baptism. Conversion is an ongoing journey.

There are no studies for Christmas Day or the Sunday following (Holy Family Sunday), because it is a holiday time and people are gathering with family and friends. There is a study for Epiphany and Baptism of our Lord. The Baptism of our Lord ends the Christmas season when we continue the routine of ordinary time.

The Word became flesh
and lived among us, . . .
full of grace and truth.

(John 1:14)

First Sunday of Advent
Year B

Opening Song

Opening Prayer

Open in prayer and invite everyone to add their own prayer. Close together: Lord, you are the potter; we are the clay, the work of your hands. Amen. (Isaiah 64:8)

Review Study Guidelines

First Reading

Isaiah 63:16-17, 64:1, 3-8 (or 15b-17, 19b-1, 2-7)

Setting the Stage

The first reading is from the book of the prophet Isaiah. Isaiah lives in about 721 B.C. The words we hear are part of a beautiful poem, one of the "jewels of the Bible."[16] It is written at the beginning of the exile, nearly 600 years before Jesus. This is the time when the Hebrew people are conquered and deported from Palestine to Babylon (modern-day Iraq). This portion of Scripture is presented as a prayer. Isaiah sees everything, both good and bad, as coming from the hand of God. Does this powerful example of trust express our feelings, too?

Read the first reading aloud. Reread this Scripture. What word, phrase, or idea stands out for you?

Exploring Further

1. What is Isaiah imploring God to remember in Isaiah 63:16 (or 15b-16)?

2. What results when God acts according to Isaiah 64:1-3 (or 19b-2)?

3. What awesome deeds has God wrought for the Israelites?
    Exodus 12:11-13
    Exodus 13:21-22
    Exodus 14:21-22, 27-28
    Exodus 24:12, 15-17

4. How does God further show His awesome power as Redeemer in Colossians 1:13-14?

5. What are we told about God in Isaiah 64:4 (or verse 3)?

6. In what way does Jesus further fulfill the Scripture, "No ear has ever heard, no eye ever seen, any God but you doing such deeds for those who wait for him"?
    Matthew 8:2-3
    Matthew 8:14-17
    Matthew 8:23-27

7. Why ought we to prepare according to Sunday's gospel, Mark 13:31-35?

8. As the servants called to watch, what does Jesus emphasize in Mark 13:36-37?

9. What do we wait and prepare for according to the following Scriptures?
    John 14:1-3
    Revelation 21:3-4

10. How does God respond to the obedient in Isaiah 64:5a (or verse 4a)?

11. What happens when we are not aware of God's presence?
    Isaiah 63:17
    Isaiah 64:5b (or verse 4b)

12. What descriptive words are used to describe sin in Isaiah 64:6-7 (or verse 5-6)?

13. What does Isaiah remind God of in Isaiah 64:8 (or verse 7)?

14. What do we learn from the following Scriptures about the roles of the potter and the clay?
    Isaiah 29:16
    Isaiah 45:9
    Jeremiah 18:1-6
    Romans 9:20-21

Reflection

1. In what situation of your life, country, or world are you waiting with hope but would like God to "tear open the heavens and come down...performing unexpected deeds"? How have you seen the power of God at work?

2. People who turn from God are described in Isaiah as unclean, their good deeds like polluted rags, withered leaves blown by the wind, not calling to God, and not clinging to God. Isaiah says God turned from His people because the people strayed from His ways, hardened their hearts, and do not reverence Him. How does this description of sin apply today? What keeps you from calling to and clinging to God? How can we keep from straying and instead grow in reverence to God's ways?

3. Which of the following scenarios best describes your current condition: pliable clay God can work with, wet clay that is not firm enough to hold the shape of the vessel, complaining clay, jealous clay, content clay, clay that knows your role, a cracked clay pot in need of repair, or trusting clay? What type of clay do you desire to be?

4. Jesus left his servants to both watch and to be prepared. How can you stay awake and not miss Jesus in your prayer time? In the events of each day?

Optional Exercise. Have each person in the group briefly share about an event from his or her past week or about an upcoming event. This could be a time to share a triumph, trial, or need.

Second Reading

1 Corinthians 1:3-9

Setting the Stage
This reading gives us the opening lines of St. Paul's first letter that he writes to the church in Corinth, Greece, about 25 years after the resurrection of Jesus. Through these words of Paul we hear God our Father telling us what He is doing for the church and what He will do for us as we wait for the second coming of Christ.

Read the second reading aloud. Reread this Scripture. What word, phrase, or idea stands out for you?

Exploring Further

1. What does Paul give thanks for in 1 Corinthians 1:4?

2. What have we been given according to 1 Corinthians 1:5-7a?

3. What are the Corinthians (and us) waiting for according to 1 Corinthians 1:7b?

4. What is God doing for us and desiring for us?
   1 Corinthians 1:8
   2 Corinthians 1:21
   Ephesians 1:4
   Colossians 1:22-23

5. God is strengthening us to be holy and blameless when Jesus returns. Why is this good news when considering Sunday's gospel, Mark 13:32-37?

6. What has God called us to in 1 Corinthians 1:9a?

7. What does fellowship with Jesus entail?
   Acts 2:42
   1 Corinthians 10:16-17
   1 Peter 4:12-16
   1 John 1:3-7
   2 John 9

8. Why can we trust God?
   1 Corinthians 1:9b
   1 Corinthians 10:13

Reflection

1. Who has helped you to be more firmly rooted in your faith? How have others encouraged you by sharing their spiritual resources and gifts with you? Place the name of those who have blessed you in Paul's prayer: "I continually thank my God for _____."

2. God is strengthening us to be holy and blameless when Christ returns. This Advent, how can we stand firm in faith? Encourage others? Fellowship with Jesus and one another in preparation for when Jesus comes again?

Closing Prayer

I wait for You, O Lord; I lift up my soul to my God. In You I trust; do not let me be disgraced; no one is disgraced who waits on You. Amen. (Psalm 25 NAB)

Second Sunday of Advent
Year B

Opening Song

Opening Prayer

Open in prayer and invite everyone to add his or her own prayer. Close together: Lord, show us how to prepare the way for Your coming into our lives anew. Amen.

Review Study Guidelines

First Reading

Isaiah 40:1-5, 9-11

Setting the Stage

The first reading is from the book of the prophet Isaiah. Isaiah lives in about 721 B.C. The Babylonians are later defeated by the Persians, whose foreign policy is very different; they allow conquered peoples to live on their soil and keep their religion. So this is a time of consolation for Judah. Note the name "Zion." It is the name of the hill on which Jerusalem, their capital, is built and is a symbol for the whole nation. Through these words, God our Father gives us a comforting image of Jesus born to be our Good Shepherd, coming to lead us home.

Read the first reading aloud. Reread this Scripture. What word, phrase, or idea stands out for you?

Exploring Further

1. Israel has a history of turning from God. They are now in exile. What message does God tell Isaiah to speak in Isaiah 40:1-2?

2. What do the following Scriptures say about preparing?
Isaiah 40:3-5
Malachi 3:1-4

3. Who fulfills this passage and how according to Sunday's gospel, Mark 1:1-6?

4. What do the following verses tell us regarding God's intent when He comes?
Isaiah 40:11
Luke 15:4-6
John 10:11, 14-16

5. What does John say about the One he prepares the way for in Mark 1:7-8?

6. What should we do with the good news of Jesus according to Isaiah 40:9-10?

Reflection

1. God is sending hope and comfort to His people. When have you experienced God's comfort in the midst of hard times? What hope were you given?

2. Building highways, raising up valleys, and levelling ground all speak of major renovations and efforts to make a well-marked road. When preparing for Jesus to return, how do we fill in fill in rough spots, remove obstacles, and create a well marked road in our lives? What role does repentance play in the preparation process?

3. "Note that the shepherd is caring for the most defenceless members of his society: children and pregnant (or nursing) women. This reinforces the prophetic theme that the truly powerful nation is not the one with a strong military, but rather the one that relies on God's caring strength."[17] In what ways does your country show strength by caring for its defenceless members? Where is more care needed? What are you doing to care for the defenceless or vulnerable members of society?

Optional Exercise. Have each person in the group briefly share about an event from his or her past week or about an upcoming event. This could be a time to share a triumph, trial, or need.

Second Reading

2 Peter 3:8-15

Setting the Stage

This reading is from the second letter of Peter, written almost 100 years after the resurrection of Jesus. Many Christians are wondering why Jesus is taking so long to come back again. This poetic picture is meant to help us catch the great feeling of that day as the Lord Jesus comes in majesty and power! What a day that will be for us! But the question is, "Does God our Father rush into things, like we so often do?"

Read the second reading aloud. Reread this Scripture. What word, phrase, or idea stands out for you?

Exploring Further

1. What do the following Scriptures suggest about God's timing and possible reasons why God is delaying His return?
    2 Peter 3:8-9
    Romans 2:4
    Isaiah 30:18
    Ezekiel 18:23

2. How will the day of the Lord come according to 2 Peter 3:10?

3. How should we be living while we wait for the day of the Lord?
    2 Peter 3:11-12, 14
    Mark 1:3-5, Sunday's gospel

4. What are we waiting for according to 2 Peter 3:13?

5. What is promised that we are waiting for in hope?
    Isaiah 60:21-22
    Isaiah 65:17-19
    Romans 8:18-25
    Hebrews 12:28-29

Reflection

1. This world as we know it will pass away. How can you keep your priorities and grow in holiness and devotion while waiting for the second coming?

2. During Advent we remember the baby Jesus coming into the world as our Saviour. And with it, we get a small taste of what it means to wait in hope for Jesus to return at the end of time as Lord and King forever. If it were up to you, would you like the return of Christ to be soon or would you like for His return to be delayed? Why?

3. How patient are you at waiting for events like holidays, weddings, the arrival of a child, during an illness, etc. Explain. How do you spend your time waiting and preparing? What is the value of waiting and preparing?

Closing Prayer

God of love and mercy, remove the things that hinder us from receiving Christ with joy. We open our hearts and make welcome our Saviour and Redeemer. Amen.

THIRD SUNDAY OF ADVENT
YEAR B

Opening Song

Opening Prayer

Open in prayer and invite everyone to add his or her own prayer. Close together: Rejoice in the Lord always; again, I say rejoice! The Lord is very near. Amen. (Philippians 3:4)

Review Study Guidelines

First Reading

Isaiah 61:1-2, 10-11

Setting the Stage
The first reading is from the book of the prophet Isaiah. These words are first spoken around 540 B.C. when the Hebrew people are beginning to return from exile in Babylon (modern-day Iraq) to their devastated capital city of Jerusalem.

Read the first reading aloud. Reread this Scripture. What word, phrase, or idea stands out for you?

Exploring Further

1. What is the prophet aware of, and what is he called to do in Isaiah 61:1a?

2. The Jewish people are expecting a Messiah. What signs proclaim His coming according to Isaiah 61:1b-3?

3. How is this Scripture from Isaiah fulfilled and by whom?
    Matthew 3:16-17
    Luke 4:16-21

4. John has been preparing the way for the Messiah and is in prison as a result. What does Jesus' message to John affirm in Matthew 11:2-6?

5. What is John sent to do according to Sunday's gospel, John 1:6-8?

6. How does John respond when asked who he is in Sunday's gospel, John 1:19-28?

7. What is the Lord praised for in Isaiah 61:10?

8. What will God cause to spring up according to Isaiah 61:11?

9. From the following Scriptures what do garments symbolize?
    Isaiah 61:10
    Zechariah 3:3-5
    Galatians 3:27
    Revelation 7:9, 13-14

Reflection

1. Have each person read aloud Isaiah 61:1 and 10, inserting his or her name in place of "me" or "I." Ask if they believe these Scriptures are true with their name in them. Why or why not?

2. Through baptism, our status as children of God is confirmed and we now share the mission of Jesus. Consider your life at this time and complete the statement: "The spirit of the Lord is upon me. He has sent me to _____."

3. In the above Scriptures, clothes symbolize garments of salvation, robes of righteousness, filthy clothes of sin, clean clothes and turbans of forgiveness, and fine linen of righteous acts. Baptism clothes us in Christ and white robes wash martyrs in the blood of Christ. What spiritual garments are you wearing? Explain.

4. What has God done for you to cause praise to sprout for all to see?

5. John was called to bear witness to Jesus and did not take any esteem for himself. How are you called to bear witness to Jesus? How can taking credit or esteem for ourselves be avoided?

Optional Exercise. Have each person in the group briefly share about an event from his or her past week or about an upcoming event. This could be a time to share a triumph, trial, or need.

Second Reading

1 Thessalonians 5:16-24

Setting the Stage

This reading is from the end of the first letter St. Paul writes to the church in Thessalonica, northern Greece, in A.D. 51. Paul mentions "prophets." The gift of "prophecy" is given to a person to speak words of encouragement and direction to the community.[18] These words of God our Father can be easily applied to us as we prepare for Christmas.

Read the second reading aloud. Reread this Scripture. What word, phrase, or idea stands out for you?

Exploring Further

1. What three things are we to do as we wait in hope for the coming of Jesus in 1 Thessalonians 5:16-18?

2. What advice is given in 1 Thessalonians 5:21?

3. In what practical ways can you hold fast to what is good?
   1 Thessalonians 5:19-20, 22
   Job 1:1
   Philippians 4:8-9
   1 John 3:18

4. What is God able to do for us according to 1 Thessalonians 5:23?

5. What reason for hope do we have in 1 Thessalonians 5:24?

Reflection

1. Which response best describes you—rejoicing, praying, giving thanks, complaining, or worrying? Can you think of a time you made a conscious decision to rejoice or pray or give thanks in the midst of an unexpected or frustrating situation? What happened?

2. Who is an example from the past who "held fast to what is good"? Do you know someone personally who has done so? How does his or her steadfastness and endurance help or encourage you?

3. St. Therese of Lisieux, toward the end of her life, had a beautiful image of salvation. She describes salvation thus:

All of her life she is a little girl. She is proud and happy to be a little girl. Her heavenly father is standing at the top of the great staircase, always beckoning her, "Come, Therese! Come! I ask more of you!" She lifts her little foot again and again by all the actions of her Catholic faith and religious life, trying to please God. She is trying to climb up to God. God watches Therese and sees her desire to come. Then in one moment that we call grace, God rushes down the staircase, picks her up and takes her. She knows afterward by hindsight that God has done it, from the beginning to end. But it was important for her to keep lifting up her little foot. Our struggle, our desire, our yes is significant and necessary. But in the end it is always grace that carries us up the staircase.[19]

- Regarding this reflection and the readings today, what would you consider to be God's part and what is your part in preparing for the coming of Jesus?

Closing Prayer

The Spirit of the Lord is upon me. He has sent me to bring good news. Lord, help me to be faithful to what You have sent me to do. Amen.

Fourth Sunday of Advent
Year B

Opening Song

Opening Prayer

Open in prayer and invite everyone to add his or her own prayer. Close together: Lord, help us to live as Your servants, allowing Your will to be accomplished through us. Amen.

Review Study Guidelines

First Reading

2 Samuel 7:1-5, 8-12, 14, 16

Setting the Stage

The first reading is from the second book of Samuel. We hear of a famous episode in the life of King David, who lived 1,000 years before Jesus. After many years of struggles, David brought the Twelve Tribes of the Hebrews into a confederation and chose Jerusalem as its capital. Things are going well; he has a fine palace to live in and the country is at peace. But there is something missing, so he discusses the problem with the prophet of the day. It is important to note that:

1. The "ark" mentioned here is not Noah's ark! The "ark of God" is the sacred wooden box that stores the precious stone tablets on which are written the Ten Commandments. The Hebrew people keep this box in a special tent as they move from place to place during their long desert journey and for a long time afterward in the Promised Land.

2. There is a play on words here: the word "house" can mean "palace," "temple," and "family."[20] David's son, Solomon, is referred to in this passage, but we are preparing to celebrate the birthday of another descendant of David who is "greater than Solomon."

Read the first reading aloud. Reread this Scripture. What word, phrase, or idea stands out for you?

Exploring Further

1. What is David's situation and his concern in 2 Samuel 7:1-2?

2. Who is the prophet at this time, what does he tell David in 2 Samuel 7:3?

3. What changes in 2 Samuel 7:4-5?

4. What does God do for David?
   2 Samuel 7:8
   1 Samuel 16:10-13

5. How is God with David according to the following Scriptures?
   2 Samuel 7:9
   1 Samuel 17:32-37
   1 Samuel 17:41-50
   1 Samuel 23:4-5

6. What does God promise David in 2 Samuel 7:10-12?

7. What will David's offspring do and what will God do according to 2 Samuel 7:13-15?

8. How is this promise to David partially fulfilled according to 1 Kings 8:17-21?

9. What does God say about the perpetuity of David's kingdom in 2 Samuel 7:16?

10. How is this promise fulfilled according to Sunday's gospel, Luke 1:26-35?

11. How is God continuing to build a temple today according to the following?
    John 14:23
    1 Corinthians 3:16-17
    1 Peter 2:5

12. David surrenders his plan to build a temple for God. In a similar way, how does Mary surrender her plans to God according to Luke 1:38?

13. What sign does God give Mary to confirm his promise in Luke 1:36-37?

    Note: The sign given to Mary in confirmation of the angel's announcement to her is the pregnancy of her aged relative Elizabeth. If a woman past the childbearing age could become pregnant, why, the angel implies, should there be doubt about Mary's pregnancy, for *nothing will be impossible for God.* [21]

Reflection

1. Nathan is the prophet during the time of King David. The role of the prophet is to urge people to follow God and to communicate God's laws and plans to the people.[22] In every age God has uses people to

communicate God's law and plans. Who do you think fulfills this role in our day? Do you listen to what these people or groups say, reject their advice, or pick and choose as you see fit? Explain.

2. David desires to do a good thing yet God says no. Have you ever worked and prayed for something that is good, yet it did not happen? Explain. God is planning something greater in David's life. Is it possible God has something greater in store for you or your group? Why or why not?

3. David can see God's hand on his life from his youth. In looking back on your life, where do you see God's hand?

4. God wants to build a home in your heart where Jesus dwells and is a place of refuge, shelter, joy, and worship. God wants you to be a living stone built into a living temple with all God's people. What does this mean to you? How can you cooperate with God in this work?

5. Letting go of our plans and agenda and accept God's plan, as David and Mary did, takes humility and faith. Can you think of a time your humility and faith have been called upon to let go of your plans and accept and trust God with His plan?

Optional Exercise. Have each person in the group briefly share about an event from his or her past week or about an upcoming event. This could be a time to share a triumph, trial, or need.

Second Reading

Romans 16:25-27

Setting the Stage

This short second reading is only one long sentence from the letter St. Paul writes to the church in Rome about 27 years after the resurrection of Jesus. In the letter, Paul explains the "mystery"—God's plan to show His love to the "Gentiles"; that is, to all the peoples of the world who are not Jewish. But He wants to do this by having the Jewish people be the channels and instruments of His peace. So, Jesus is born a Jew and is God our Father's finest messenger. With St. Paul we offer our praise.

Read the second reading aloud. Reread this Scripture. What word, phrase, or idea stands out for you?

Exploring Further

1. This short reading is called a doxology, which is a hymn or prayer of thanksgiving. What does Paul say God is able to do for you in Romans 16:25?

2. What do the following Scriptures say God will do for believers?
   1 Corinthians 1:8
   2 Corinthians 1:21-22
   2 Thessalonians 3:3
   Jude 24-25

3. How is this mystery being made known?
   Romans 16:26
   Matthew 28:16-20
   Ephesians 3:8-12
   Colossians 1:25-27

4. What revelation of this mystery is made known to us?
   Ephesians 1:7-10
   2 Timothy 1:9-10
   1 Peter 1:20-21
   Luke 1:30-35, Sunday's gospel

5. How is God described in Romans 16:27?

6. How is God's wisdom described in 1 Corinthians 1:21-25?

Reflection

1. In the above Scriptures we hear that when we accept the gospel of Jesus Christ, God will make us strong in faith, strengthen our faith to stand firm, keep us from, falling, make us strong to the end, and make us blameless before Christ. He encourages our hearts, strengthens us for every good word and deed, and protects us from evil. In which of these areas do you need God to strengthen you today? Which of these do we need as we try to live for Christ in our current culture?

2. The "mystery" from the beginning of time is salvation through the death and resurrection of Jesus. Through this event, death is destroyed and eternal life is made possible. We are redeemed, forgiven, and we can set our hope on God. In today's readings, this is referred to as the "wisdom of God." Why do you think God's plan seems foolish or a stumbling block for many? Is this mystery hard for you to believe? Explain. Why does God unfold this mystery over centuries?

3. Romans 16:26 says the mystery is revealed to bring about the "obedience of faith." (Faith is to believe; obedience is to live out what we believe.) What obedience do you think your faith calls you to in light of today's Scriptures?

4. Paul is excited to be alive and share in the work when God's mystery of salvation is being made known to the world. We too live in a time when the plan of salvation is being made known to the world. Does this excite you? Is his a work you want to be involved in? Why or why not? How do you or have you shared in making known the plan of salvation?

Closing Prayer

Lord, give us the strength of faith to stand firm in You, hope in You, and proclaim You. Amen.

Epiphany of Our Lord
Year B

Opening Song

Opening Prayer

Open in prayer and invite everyone to add his or her own prayer. Close together: King and Saviour, You are the light and truth made manifest to all nations. Lord, please grant us an encounter of this revelation in our lives today. Amen.

Review Study Guidelines

First Reading

Isaiah 60:1-6

Setting the Stage

The first reading is from the book of the prophet Isaiah. These words are spoken about 540 years before Jesus. The Jewish people have been conquered 50 years earlier by the Babylonians, Jerusalem has been destroyed, and many are deported to Babylon (modern-day Iraq). However, the Babylonians are conquered by the Persian Empire, whose foreign policy is very different; they allow conquered peoples to have their own customs and religion and to live in their own country. So the deported Jews are going home at last. This reading is a poem addressed to the people of Jerusalem who have been left there when the deportations took place. We shall be hearing in this reading the ancient names for Arabia, Ethiopia, and Spain. Through these words, God our Father tells us who are called to be His people.

Read the first reading aloud. Reread this Scripture. What word, phrase, or idea stands out for you?

Exploring Further

1. What is promised to the Israelites?
    Isaiah 60:1-2
    Matthew 2:4-5, Sunday's gospel

2. How will other nations be affected by this promise?
    Isaiah 60:3
    Isaiah 42:1, 4
    Micah 4:1-3

3. How is the rising star that leads nations fulfilled in Sunday's gospel, Matthew 2:1-2, 9-10?

4. How does Herod react to the news the Magi bring in Matthew 2:3, 7-8, 13?

5. What is promised to Israel in Isaiah 60:4?

6. How will Israel be honoured by other nations?
    Isaiah 60:5-6
    Psalm 72:10-11

7. How is the promise of nations bringing wealth and paying homage fulfilled in Matthew 2:11?

8. The gift of gold represents royalty, the frankincense represents divinity, and myrrh indicates passion or suffering. In presenting gold, frankincense, and myrrh to Jesus, what are the wise men indicating about this baby in the stable?

9. After the star leads the wise men to Jesus, they pay homage and present gifts, how do the Magi return home and why in Matthew 2:12?

Reflection

1. Jesus is the light promised to all nations. Epiphany is the manifestation of God to all peoples. What is the truth Jesus brings that transcends all time, all nations, and all cultures to meet the need of every human heart?

2. Isaiah speaks of the overflowing joy in Israel in seeing their sons and daughters return from captivity. What things today consign people in captivity? Can you relate to the joy of being freed from captivity in your life or in seeing someone else's life healed and transformed? Explain.

3. The wise men presented Jesus with gifts or treasure. What gifts or treasure do you have to present to Jesus directly or to give to others?

4. After the wise men's encounter with the living God, they return home by a different route. After searching and encountering Jesus, we are never the same. How has your life taken a different route since an encounter with the living God?

Optional Exercise. Have each person in the group briefly share about an event from his or her past week or about an upcoming event. This could be a time to share a triumph, trial, or need.

Second Reading

Ephesians 3:2-3, 5-6

Setting the Stage

The second reading is from the letter of Paul to the Ephesians. This is a circular letter to the Christians living around Ephesus (modern-day southwestern Turkey). Scholars are uncertain about the actual author. It is either Paul or one of his followers who, under the inspiration of the Holy Spirit, take Paul's thoughts and life experiences and record them under Paul's name toward the end of the A.D. first century. In any case, these are God our Father's words and He tells us about St. Paul, a fervent Jew who is touched by Jesus about six years after His resurrection. We hear why this happens.

Read the second reading aloud. Reread this Scripture. What word, phrase, or idea stands out for you?

Exploring Further

1. What is Paul reminding his listeners of in Ephesians 3:2-3?

2. What is Paul's commission according to Ephesians 3:7-8?

3. How does Paul receive revelation of this mystery in Acts 26:12-18?

4. How is this mystery revealed according to Ephesians 3:4-5?

5. What does the mystery of the gospel being revealed mean to the Gentiles in Ephesians 3:6?

6. With whom does God share the mystery of Jesus' birth?
   Matthew 2:1-2, 9-11, Sunday's gospel
   Luke 2:8-16
   Luke 2:25-32

7. What should be a guiding star for us according to 2 Peter 1:16-19?

Reflection

1. Paul is commissioned to bring the mystery of the gospel to the Gentiles so that all people can share in the promises of Jesus Christ. In your life, what have you been commissioned to or given the privilege of doing for the sake of the gospel?

2. The prophets and apostles are given revelation of the mystery of the gospel by the Holy Spirit. God reveals the birth of Jesus to the shepherds, the wise men who are strangers and foreigners, and Simeon. What characteristics do these people have that make them open to God's revelation? What attitudes should we develop to be fertile soil to receive from God?

3. The wise men followed the star that led them to Jesus. What is your star that led you, or is leading you, to Jesus?

Closing Prayer

Lord, thank You for making it possible for us to share in all the promises of Jesus Christ. Give us the grace to seek and follow the stars You lead us by. Amen.

BAPTISM OF OUR LORD
YEAR B

Opening Song

Opening Prayer

Open in prayer and invite everyone to add his or her own prayer. Close together: Lord, we seek You with all our hearts. We call on You and turn to You for mercy. Amen.

Review Study Guidelines

First Reading

Isaiah 55:1-11

Setting the Stage

The first reading is from the book of the prophet Isaiah. These words are spoken after the Hebrew people have been deported to Babylon (modern-day Iraq) at the beginning of the sixth century B.C. God our Father promises them that they will return, and they do—50 years later! But we ask:

1. Why does He allow so much suffering? What are His thoughts?
2. He kept His word to the Hebrew people; will He do the same for us?
3. Can it be that He, Himself, is strength and nourishment?

Read the first reading aloud. Reread this Scripture. What word, phrase, or idea stands out for you?

Exploring Further

1. What invitation does God present in the follow passages?
   Isaiah 55:1-2
   Proverbs 9:5-6

2. God invites us to come to the water. What does water symbolize?
   Isaiah 12:3
   Proverbs 13:14
   Sirach 24:23-31 (or verse 22-29) (See appendix one)
   John 7:37-39
   Revelation 22:17

3. How does Jesus say this invitation is fulfilled in John 6:35?

4. What four actions to God's invitation are mentioned in Isaiah 55:1, 3, 6?

5. What promise does God renew?
   Isaiah 55:3-5
   Jeremiah 32:40-41

6. What covenant does God make with David in 2 Samuel 7:10-12, 16?

7. How is this promise to David fulfilled in Acts 13:32-34?

8. To receive this promise, what must we do?
   Isaiah 55:6-7
   Zechariah 1:3
   Mark 1:15
   John 3:5

9. Who prepares the way for those to be born with water and the Spirit according to Sunday's gospel, Mark 1:6-8?

10. Why do we need to turn to God according to Isaiah 55:8-9?

11. How does God respond when we turn to Him?
    Psalm 103:10-13
    Luke 15:20

12. What does God say about His Word in Isaiah 55:10-11?

13. When the opportunity to repent and heed God's Word is refused, what is the result in Amos 8:11-12?

Reflection

1. What do people desire that leaves them empty or disappointed? How have you been thirsty or hungry for the things of God? What would a famine of God's Word look like?

2. It [water] symbolises also the life imparted by divine Wisdom and by the Law. This symbolism is carried further in the gospel narrative: living water signifies the Spirit[23] How can we "drink" from God? How do we come, hear, and seek as we are encouraged to in Isaiah?

3. In seeking and turning to God, why is it essential to repent and believe, turn to God for mercy, forsake wickedness, and be born of water and the Spirit? How is this part of your life?

4. Just as the rain and snow water the earth and cause growth, so too God's Word waters the earth and achieves God's purpose and desires. How have you experienced God's Word working in your life? What opportunities do you have to sow the Word of Life in the lives of others?

Optional Exercise. Have each person in the group briefly share about an event from his or her past week or about an upcoming event. This could be a time to share a triumph, trial, or need.

Second Reading

1 John 5:1-9

Setting the Stage

The next reading is from the first letter of John. This is written around A.D. 90 to the Christians who are close to St. John the Apostle. God our Father tells us why our faith in Jesus is so important, and He tells us how we can know Jesus is His Son. Note these words:
1. He "came by water" is a reference to the baptism of Jesus.
2. He "came by blood" refers to the shedding of His blood and His dying on the cross.

Read the second reading aloud. Reread this Scripture. What word, phrase, or idea stands out for you?

Exploring Further

1. What happens when we believe in Jesus according to 1 John 5:1a?

2. What is the result of loving the Father in 1 John 5:1b?

3. What is the proof of loving the Father and His children according to 1 John 5:2-3?

4. How is the above Scripture summed up in 1 John 3:23-24?

5. What does our faith enable us to do according to 1 John 5:4? (See appendix two)

6. Who conquers the world according to 1 John 5:5?

7. Instead of being burdensome, what results when we follow God's commands?
   Deuteronomy 30:11-16
   Matthew 11:28-30
   John 16:33

8. How many witnesses are required to testify in Jewish law?
   Deuteronomy 17:6
   John 8:17

9. The testimony of Christ is confirmed by what three witnesses in 1 John 5:6-9?

10. How do the water, spirit, and blood give testimony in the following?
    Mark 1:9-10, Sunday's gospel
    John 14:26
    John 19:34

The blood shows that the lamb has truly been sacrificed for the salvation of the world, the water, symbol of the Spirit, shows the sacrifice is a rich source of grace. Many of the Fathers interpret the water and the blood as symbols of baptism and the Eucharist, and these two sacraments as signifying the Church, which is born like a second Eve from the side of another Adam.[24]

Water and blood refers to Christ's baptism and to the shedding of his blood on the cross. The *Spirit* was present at the baptism. The *testimony* to Christ as the Son of God is confirmed by divine witness, greater by far than the two legally required human witnesses....The gist of the divine witness or *testimony* is that *eternal* life is given in Christ and nowhere else. To *possess the Son* is not acceptance of a doctrine but of a person who lives now and provides life.[25]

Reflection

1. Your "divine sonship" is affirmed at your baptism. Were you baptized as a child or as an adult or not at all? What are the advantages of baptism as a child? As an adult? If you haven't been baptized, are you considering it? Why or why not? What does being a child of God mean to you? What are the privileges and responsibilities of baptism?

2. All who believe in Jesus Christ are children of God. All believers are your family members. If we believe in Jesus and love God, we *must* love one another. Is this hard or easy for you? Explain. What is the evidence of your love for believers, especially those outside your immediate circle?

3. Practical faith as described in this reading has the power to overcome evil. Think to yourself of an area you struggle with. In what practical ways can you apply your faith in Jesus to overcome and receive redemption?

Closing Prayer

Lord, because of our belief in You, we are family. Help us to value one another as You do. We trust that Your power working in us is enough to stand firm and conquer evil with You. Amen.

SECTION THREE
ORDINARY TIME AFTER CHRISTMAS

The baptism of Jesus ends the Christmas season, and we are back into the routine of ordinary time.

Remember that ordinary time is an ideal time to develop a solid foundation and a relationship with the Father, Son, and Holy Spirit that will prepare us for the times of celebration as well as the times of sorrow.

Easter is a moveable feast day which means the number of Sundays of Ordinary Time between now and Lent varies from five to nine. "At the Council of Nicaea in 325, all Churches agreed that Easter, the Christian Passover, should be celebrated on the Sunday following the first full moon after the vernal [spring] equinox."[26] Watch for the first Sunday of Lent.

You show me the path of life.
In your presence there is
fullness of joy...

(Psalm 16:11)

Second Sunday of Ordinary Time
Year B

Opening Song

Opening Prayer

Open in prayer and invite everyone to add his or her own prayer. Close together: Lord, speak to us, Your people. Your servants are listening. Amen.

Review Study Guidelines

First Reading

1 Samuel 3:3-10, 19

Setting the Stage

The reading is from the first book of Samuel. Samuel is a prophet who lives 1,000 years before Jesus. In this reading we hear of an event that takes place when Samuel is a boy helping a man called Eli, the priest in charge of the temple in Shiloh, which is about 20 miles north of Jerusalem. This is before the great temple of Jerusalem is built. The ark referred to here is the sacred wooden box, 4 feet by 2 feet by 2 feet that holds the two precious stone tablets on which are written the Ten Commandments. We hear how Samuel gets his vocation to be a prophet. As we read these Scriptures, we need to be asking ourselves how we will respond if God our Father calls us.

Read the first reading aloud. Reread this Scripture. What word, phrase, or idea stands out for you?

Exploring Further

1. Where is Samuel sleeping and what is present there in 1 Samuel 3:3?

2. What does God do for Moses in the presence of the ark in Exodus 25:22?

3. What information concerning the "lamp of God" do we discover in Exodus 27:20-21? How is this practice carried on in Catholic churches today?

4. How does God call Samuel and how does he respond in 1 Samuel 3:4-6?

5. In the following Scriptures, what is the result when the Lord calls people by name?
   Isaiah 6:1-8
   Jeremiah 1:4-10
   John 1:42, Sunday's gospel
   John 20:15-17
   Acts 22:6-8, 10

6. Why is it understandable that Eli does not realize that it is God calling Samuel from the information given in 1 Samuel 3:1?

7. What reason is given for Samuel not recognizing the Lord calling in 1 Samuel 3:7?

8. What does Eli perceive and how does he tell Samuel to respond in 1 Samuel 3:8-9?

9. What does John perceive and how do his disciples respond in Sunday's gospel, John 1:35-39?

10. After hearing and encountering Jesus, what does Andrew do in John 1:40-41?

11. What is the first prophetic word Samuel receives in 1 Samuel 3:10-14?

12. What indicates this is a difficult message for Samuel in 1 Samuel 3:15-18, and how does Eli respond?

13. How is God present with Samuel according to 1 Samuel 3:19?

Reflection

1. When Jesus spoke Mary's name, she recognizes him; then Mary is sent with a message for the disciples. Samuel's ears were opened to receive prophesy; he is then given a hard word to deliver to Eli. Simon is given a new name; then he left everything to follow Jesus. Saul is renamed Paul; then he must trust those he persecuted, repent, and go on to witness and preach. Do you believe the Lord personally calls you by name? What action in your life resulted from an encounter with Jesus?

2. Samuel is not familiar with the Lord, because the Lord has not revealed Himself to him yet (verse 7). Isaiah and Jeremiah are afraid when they encountered God and responded, "I can't." God enables them to serve anyway. How do you think God's grace and timing play a part in our response? What might this mean for those you pray for who seem to have no interest in God?

3. After Andrew hears and encounters Jesus, he brings his brother to Jesus. How can we bring others to Jesus?

Optional Exercise. Have each person in the group briefly share about an event from his or her past week or about an upcoming event. This could be a time to share a triumph, trial, or need.

Second Reading

Corinthians 6:13-15, 17-20

Setting the Stage

The next reading is from the first letter Paul writes to the church in Corinth, Greece, when he is in Ephesus (modern-day southwestern Turkey), about 25 years or so after the resurrection of Jesus. Reports have come to him that there are serious problems in Corinth, and one is about sexuality. Some Christians are saying that sexual intercourse is as necessary for the body as eating and drinking, and that there are no limits to sexual behaviour. Note that the meaning of the word *fornication* is both premarital and extramarital sex. Through these words of Paul, God our Father is telling us why sexual intercourse is so special.

Read the second reading aloud. Reread this Scripture. What word, phrase, or idea stands out for you?

Exploring Further

1. What important principle for all desires does Paul express?
   1 Corinthians 6:12
   Galatians 5:1

2. In response to those saying sexual intercourse is as important as food, Paul states that food is for this world. In contrast, what does our sexual conduct affect and what will become of our bodies?
   1 Corinthians 6:13-14
   Colossians 2:11-12

3. What do the following Scriptures teach regarding Christianity' being a physical religion and the importance of the body?
   Genesis 1:27-28, 31
   John 1:14

4. What value does God give our bodies?
   1 Corinthians 6:15a, 19
   1 Corinthians 12:27

5. What spiritual reality takes place through sexual intercourse in 1 Corinthians 6:15-16?

6. What is God's plan for sexual intercourse as explained in the following Scriptures?
   Genesis 2:23-24
   Tobit 8:4-9 (See appendix one)
   Proverbs 5:15-20
   Song of Solomon 4:10-5:4
   1 Corinthians 7:3-5

7. What does the oneness of marriage reflect?
   Ephesians 5:25-31
   Revelation 19:7

8. When do we become one flesh with Jesus according to John 6:53-56?

9. As believers, what is our relationship with Christ according to 1 Corinthians 6:17?

10. Because we are members of the body of Christ and are one spirit with Christ, what should be avoided and why?
    1 Corinthians 6:18-19
    1 Corinthians 3:16

11. Who do we belong to and why?
    1 Corinthians 6:20
    Romans 3:23-25a

12. Since Christ bought us from slavery with His blood, how should we use our bodies?
    1 Corinthians 6:20b
    1 Thessalonians 4:3-7

Reflection

1. "There are numerous ways to describe God's love, but four qualities stand out. God's love is free, total, faithful, and fruitful. Another name for this kind of love is marriage. Yes, God created the sexual union so we could mirror the beauty and glory of his own eternal, life-giving love!"[27] In what ways do sexually moral lives, chaste lives, faithful marriages, self-giving, holiness, and self-control bless our society? How have you been blessed by others living out these qualities?

2. "The painful difficulties we experience in coming to terms with our sexuality do not stem from the nature of sexuality, but from sin."[28] Which of the following qualities of love: a) free, b) total, c) faithful, or d) fruitful, is violated in the following common sins: Adultery? Premarital sex? Rape? Masturbation? Artificial contraception? Pornography? Fantasy? Homosexuality?

3. When dealing with sin we have three choices: indulge, repress and deny, or acknowledge and take it to Jesus for redemption. When dealing with a sexual sin (or any sin) how might taking it to Jesus for redemption be done in a practical and ongoing way?

4. We are made in the image and likeness of God, our bodies are God's temple, and we are the body of Christ. When God bestows this value on us, how ought we to treat others? In what practical ways can we demonstrate to others that they are valuable?

Closing Prayer

Lord, we desire to do Your will and live in Your grace and truth. Let our lives be a faithful reflection of You. Amen.

THIRD SUNDAY OF ORDINARY TIME
YEAR B

Opening Song

Opening Prayer

Open in prayer and invite everyone to add his or her own prayer. Close together: The kingdom of God is near. Repent and believe the good news. Amen.

Review Study Guidelines

First Reading

Jonah 3:1-5, 10

Setting the Stage

The first reading is from the book of the prophet Jonah. The book of Jonah is like a parable, written about 350 years before Jesus. Jonah has been asked by God our Father to go tell the people of Nineveh that they will be forgiven if they ask. Nineveh is the capital city of the Assyrians who are very cruel to the Hebrews. Jonah refuses to go eastward to give them the good news; instead he goes westward, that is, he gets on a boat to cross the Mediterranean Sea headed for Tarshish (modern-day Spain). A big storm hits the boat and Jonah gets thrown overboard, where he is swallowed by a big fish that swims back eastward and spits him out on the shore where he started. Today's reading gives us "the rest of the story."

Read the first reading aloud. Reread this Scripture. What word, phrase, or idea stands out for you?

Exploring Further

1. What does God ask Jonah to do and how does Jonah respond in Jonah 3:1-3?

2. What is Jonah's first response to this request according to Jonah 1:3?

3. What happens when Jonah runs from God in Jonah 1:4, 10-2:1?

4. What is Jonah's message to the people of Nineveh in Jonah 3:4?

5. What does Jesus proclaim in Sunday's gospel, Mark 1:14-15?

6. What cities does God destroy and why in Genesis 18:20, 19:12-13, 24-25?

7. How is God's view of sin expressed in Genesis 6:5-6?

   Note: God's "regret" is a human way of expressing the fact that tolerance of sin is incompatible with his sanctity.[29]

8. What is the response of the Ninevites to Jonah's warning in Jonah 3:5-9?

9. When the people repent, what does God do according to Jonah 3:10?

10. How does Jonah react to God being merciful to the Ninevites in Jonah 4:1-2?

11. What invitation does Jesus extend and what is the response in Sunday's gospel, Mark 1:16-20?

12. What does Jesus tell the Israelites in Luke 11:29-32 and how might this same comparison apply today?

Reflection

1. Jonah is given a second chance after running from God. Can you think of a time God or another person gave you a second chance? What did you do with it?

2. Jonah sees Nineveh as the enemy and wants them destroyed. He does not want God to show them mercy. Do you see any dangers in our world today in which certain people groups or certain countries think God is with them and not others? Explain. How does this attitude line up with God's message of His mercy when we repent and believe? Can you relate to Jonah's anger because God gives mercy to the ones whom Jonah thought deserved to be destroyed? Explain.

3. Jesus proclaimed the good news as, "Repent and believe." Sin and holiness are incompatible. The Ninevites recognized their sin and believed God could destroy them, and so they repented and turned from evil. What results when people want God in their life but do not want to turn from sin to holiness? Why must repentance and belief go together?

4. Jesus called Simon, Andrew, James, and John. They left everything and followed him. When we repent and believe, what must we leave behind in order to follow Jesus?

Optional Exercise. Have each person in the group briefly share about an event from his or her past week or about an upcoming event. This could be a time to share a triumph, trial, or need.

Second Reading

1 Corinthians 7:29-31

Setting the Stage

The next reading is from the first letter of St. Paul, written about 25 years after Jesus, to the church in Corinth, Greece. This brief reading is about the shortness of life. There are some statements that seem rather strange, but keep in mind the question being dealt with: Will your current actions and possessions last forever?

Read the second reading aloud. Reread this Scripture. What word, phrase, or idea stands out for you?

Exploring Further

1. We live in the period between Jesus coming as man and the second coming of Jesus. What do the following Scriptures say about this time?
   1 Corinthians 7:29a
   2 Corinthians 6:2
   Mark 1:14-15, Sunday's gospel

2. What should our attitude be while waiting according to 1 Corinthians 7:29b-31?

   Paul advises Christians to go about the ordinary activities of life in a manner different from those who are totally immersed in them and unaware of their transitoriness.[30]

3. What attitude should we have as we await the coming of Jesus?
   Philippians 3:20
   Colossians 4:5-6
   2 Corinthians 6:2-10
   1 Peter 1:17
   1 Peter 4:7

4. What must we leave to God during this time before Christ's return?
   1 Corinthians 4:5
   Romans 12:19

5. What is important to remember?
   1 Corinthians 7:31b
   1 John 2:15-17

Reflection

1. Our time here on earth is short. Now is the time to repent and believe; now is the time of salvation. We are to use our situation in life and all we have and all the circumstances we encounter to prepare for our eternity. How might we do that?

2. Our citizenship is in heaven. Earth is passing away. How do we work and provide for ourselves and our families in a way that reflects these realities?

3. This week is also the *Week of Christian Unity*. In light of the above Scriptures, we are to leave judgment and revenge to God, live with reverence and fear of the Lord, be clear minded and self-controlled, be wise and make the most of every opportunity, persevere in hardship and rejoice in suffering. What difference would this kind of attitude and action make toward bringing about Christian unity? How can you apply one of these actions in your life this week?

Closing Prayer

Lord, bind us together in love and let the peace of Christ rule our hearts. May Your word dwell richly in us giving us wisdom and gratitude. Amen.

Fourth Sunday of Ordinary Time
Year B

Opening Song

Opening Prayer

Open in prayer and invite everyone to add his or her own prayer. Close together: Lord we want to hear Your voice today. Harden not our hearts toward You. Amen.

Review Study Guidelines

First Reading

Deuteronomy 18:15-20

Setting the Stage

The second reading is from the book of Deuteronomy. This book shows Moses speaking to the Hebrew people just before they enter the Promised Land around 1300 B.C. He is reminding them of what happened at Mount Sinai, also called "Horeb," where the Ten Commandments are given in the midst of thunder and lightning. Hearing the voice of God was a frightening experience, so the Israelites say they prefer having only human voices instead. Does God our Father want to speak to us through human beings?

Read the first reading aloud. Reread this Scripture. What word, phrase, or idea stands out for you?

Exploring Further

1. What have other nations done that God warns against in Deuteronomy 18:14?

2. What will God do and why according to Deuteronomy 18:15-17?

3. How is Moses chosen as a prophet and why according to Exodus 3:7-12?

4. How is Jesus the Son of God given the role of prophet in Matthew 17:5?

5. How does God speak to His people and what do they ask in Deuteronomy 5:22-29?

6. What comparisons are made between Jesus and Moses in the following?
    John 3:14
    John 6:14, 30-33
    Hebrews 3:1-6

7. What is God's promise in Deuteronomy 18:18a?

8. What are the Jews waiting for according to Acts 3:22-23?

9. What do these Scriptures tell us about the role of the prophet?
    Deuteronomy 18:18b-20
    Jeremiah 14:14-16
    Ezekiel 3:17-19
    Acts 3:18

10. What effect do the words Jesus speaks have according to John 12:50?

11. How can we recognize a word that the Lord has not spoken according to Deuteronomy 18:21-22?

12. What has God given us as a pillar and foundation for discerning truth according to 1 Timothy 3:15?

13. What aspect of Jesus is like a prophet in Sunday's gospel, Mark 1:21-22?

14. What demonstrates that Jesus is more than a prophet in Mark 1:23-28?

Reflection

1. In the time of Moses, people are interested in soothsayers and diviners, but God did not permit His people to seek out these things. Today there is also an interest in such things. Do you think it is acceptable for believers to partake in fortune-telling, horoscopes, crystals, diviners, soothsayers, etc.? Why or why not?

2. God speaks words of truth through His prophets. Yet frequently people do not listen. God sent His son Jesus to speak the words of truth, yet frequently we do not listen and obey. Why is it so hard to listen and obey? What areas of your life do you need to bring into obedience to God's Word?

3. What happened to most of God's prophets in Scripture? Who would you consider a prophet in the world today?

4. By virtue of our baptism, we are called to be prophets. How do you think we are meant to live this out?

Optional Exercise. Have each person in the group briefly share about an event from his or her past week or about an upcoming event. This could be a time to share a triumph, trial, or need.

Second Reading

1 Corinthians 7:17, 32-35

Setting the Stage

The next reading is from the first letter of St. Paul to the church in Corinth, Greece. He writes it about 25 years after the resurrection of Jesus. Paul is responding to reports of problems with the sexual behavior of some of the Corinthians. Paul, who is a single person, points out some of the advantages of celibacy. God our Father speaks now to all of us, no matter what our vocation is, about our common calling.

Read the second reading. Reread this Scripture. What word, phrase, or idea stands out for you?

Exploring Further

1. What basic principle is given to the new convert regarding his life circumstances at the time of conversion in 1 Corinthians 7:17, 20?

2. What advantage is there for the unmarried man in 1 Corinthians 7:32-33?

3. What is the advantage for the unmarried woman according to 1 Corinthians 7:34?

4. What reason for celibacy is given in Matthew 19:12?

5. What is Paul's purpose for promoting celibacy as expressed in 1 Corinthians 7:35?

6. What do we discover about marriage after the resurrection in Matthew 22:30?

7. What marriage will take place according to Revelation 19:7?

Reflection

1. Did your conversion to Christ (or personal epiphany or time of growth in faith) cause immediate changes to your life circumstances? (For example, married state, where you lived, schooling, job, etc.) Did it cause changes over time? Explain.

2. Paul encourages each person to lead the life that the Lord has assigned. How has your state in life, married or single, assisted you in serving Christ and His church? How has it restricted or altered what you do for Christ and His church?

3. Consider Christopher West's' reflection on celibacy:

Christ points us "back to the future" when every human longing for love and communion will be fulfilled super-abundantly in the "Marriage of the Lamb." Celibacy is not a rejection of sexuality, but a living out of its ultimate meaning.[31] As we read in the gospel, Christ calls some of his followers to embrace celibacy, not for celibacy's sake, but "for the sake of the kingdom" (Matthew 19:12). "The kingdom" is precisely the *heavenly marriage*. In short, those who choose celibacy are "skipping" the sacrament in anticipation of the real thing. By expressing the "I do" of a marriage commitment directly to God, celebates step beyond the dimension of history—while living within the dimension of history—and dramatically declare to the world the kingdom of God is here (Matthew 12:28).

We can't escape the call of our sexuality. Every man, by virtue of the fact that he is a man, is called to be a husband and father; and every woman, by virtue of the fact that she is a woman, is called to be a wife and mother—either through marriage or the celibate vocation. Celibate men become the "icon" of Christ; their bride is the church. Celibate women become the "icon" of the church; their bridegroom is Christ. And both bear many spiritual children. Thus the terms father, mother, sister, and brother are applicable to marriage and celibacy. Both vocations are indispensable to building the family of God. Each vocation complements the other and demonstrates the other's meaning. Marriage reveals the nuptial character of celibacy, and celibacy reveals that the ultimate purpose of marriage is to prepare us for heaven.[32]

- What understanding does this reflection give you regarding the role of celibacy? Do you see celibacy as a gift to the church? Why or why not?

4. Consider the relationship of celibacy, sex, and marriage. In history, what results when any of these three is overvalued, undervalued, or in anyway disrespected? How are celibacy, sex, and marriage interrelated and interdependent?

Closing Prayer

Let Your face shine on Your servant, and save me by Your love. Lord, keep me from shame, for I have called to You. Amen.

PRESENTATION OF THE LORD
ONLY WHEN SUNDAY FALLS ON FEBRUARY 2

Opening Song

Opening Prayer

Open in prayer and invite everyone to add his or her own prayer. Close together: Lord, create in me a clean heart, O God, and put a new and right spirit within me. The sacrifice acceptable to God is a broken contrite spirit; a broken and contrite heart, O God, You will not despise. Amen. (Psalm 51:10, 17)

Review Study Guidelines

First Reading

Malachi 3:1-4

Setting the Stage

The first reading is from the book of the prophet Malachi. Malachi is not a name; it is the Hebrew word for "My messenger," but we know only a little about the messenger who wrote this part of the Bible. He lives about 500 years before Jesus, and he loves his Jewish faith so much that he is not afraid to criticize the "descendents of Levi," who are the Jewish priests and temple assistants. These words are appropriately chosen for this feast of the Presentation of the Lord. We hear what a difference He will make in the temple.

Read the first reading aloud. Reread this Scripture. What word, phrase, or idea stands out for you?

Exploring Further

1. Who is God sending and for what purpose according to Malachi 3:1a?

2. Who is this messenger according to Malachi 3:23 (or Malachi 4:5)?

3. What does Jesus say about this messenger?
   Matthew 11:10-15
   Matthew 17:11-13

4. What is foretold about John the Baptist in Luke 1:11-13, 17?

5. After the way is prepared, who will enter the temple and how in Malachi 3:1?

6. How does the Lord enter the temple according to Luke 2:22-24?

7. How is the coming of Jesus to the temple announced in Luke 2:25-32, Sunday's gospel?

8. What image of the Lord's coming is given in Malachi 3:2-3?

9. What do we learn of this purifying process from the following Scriptures?
   Ezekiel 22:18-22
   Daniel 12:10
   Matthew 3:10-12
   Luke 2:33-35, Sunday's gospel

10. What are some things we need to be purified from in Malachi 3:5?

11. What will follow this purification according to Malachi 3:3b-4?

12. What type of sacrifice does God desire according to Psalm 51:17?

13. What sacrifice do we share in for the forgiveness of our sins in Hebrews 10:8-10?

Reflection

1. Who has been a "messenger" in your life preparing the way for experiencing God in a deeper way or who has been an instrument to show you your need to repent?

2. God wants to refine and purify our hearts. In what ways might this process be accomplished?

3. When the King of Glory enters the temple as a baby, only Anna and Simeon recognize him. How can we be alert to the presence of Jesus? What may cause us to not recognize His presence in our midst?

4. Simeon declared he now could be dismissed in peace for his eyes had seen salvation prepared for all people. What hope, dream, or desire fulfilled would allow you to be dismissed from this life in peace?

Optional Exercise. Have each person in the group briefly share about an event from his or her past week or about an upcoming event. This could be a time to share a triumph, trial, or need.

Second Reading

Hebrews 2:10-11, 13b-18

Setting the Stage

The next reading is from the letter to the Hebrews written by a Jewish Christian to other Jewish Christians about 40 years after the resurrection of Jesus. He often quotes from the Old Testament (and here we have a text from the prophet Isaiah). This is to show that everything in the Jewish faith points to Jesus, and to be a Christian, then, is to be a descendant of Abraham. Through this reading, God our Father tells us why Jesus became a human and then He tells us the cost for doing so.

Read the second reading aloud. Reread this Scripture. What word, phrase, or idea stands out for you?

Exploring Further

1. Why does Jesus become human (flesh and blood) according to Hebrews 2:14-15?

2. What power does Satan have according to the following Scriptures?
   Hebrews 2:14
   2 Corinthians 4:4
   1 John 5:18-19

3. What does Jesus do to Satan's power and dominion?
   Colossians 1:13-14
   2 Timothy 1:10

4. What promise does this fulfill in Isaiah 41:8-10?

5. Why did Jesus become like us?
   Hebrews 2:17
   Hebrews 4:15
   1 John 2:2

6. How is Jesus tested and why according to Hebrews 2:18?

7. Why does God test His people?
   Exodus 16:4
   Exodus 20:20
   Deuteronomy 8:2-3
   2 Chronicles 32:30-31

8. How is temptation often initiated?
   1 Thessalonians 3:5
   1 Timothy 6:9
   James 1:13-14
   Revelation 2:10

9. What is helpful to remember in times of suffering and testing?
   1 Corinthians 10:13
   1 Peter 1:6-7

Reflection

1. What does it mean to you that the power of death is destroyed?

2. How has someone's experience of suffering been an example or an encouragement to you or given you hope in your time of suffering?

3. What have you learned through suffering? How has suffering strengthened you or changed you?

Closing Prayer

Lord, we are grateful that You have shared in all our sufferings and will help us when we are tested. Give us wisdom and grace to support others in their time of suffering. Help us always turn to You and trust Your promise that You will not give us more than we can bear. Amen.

Fifth Sunday of Ordinary Time
Year B

Opening Song

Opening Prayer

Open in prayer and invite everyone to add his or her own prayer. Close together: Praise the Lord, who heals the brokenhearted. We place all our hope in You. Amen.

Review Study Guidelines

First Reading

Job 7:1-4, 6-7

Setting the Stage

The reading is from the book of Job. This is a famous poem, a literary masterpiece, written by a Jew about 500 years before Jesus. The main character is called Job, a righteous man, who believes in God our Father but who suffers deeply and does not understand why his life is full of distress. We hear him describe how he feels about his life, and we hear him pray. Do these words describe what our life is like sometimes?

Read the first reading aloud. Reread this Scripture. What word, phrase, or idea stands out for you?

Exploring Further

1. How does Job see life according to Job 7:1-3?

2. How is a similar sentiment to life, as Job conveys it, expressed in Sirach 40:1? (See appendix one)

3. What reason for life being hard is given in Genesis 3:11, 16-19?

4. How does Job describe his days and nights according to Job 7:4?

5. How does Job describe life in Job 7:6-7?

6. What similar sentiment does David express in Psalm 89:47 (or verse 48)?

7. Despite feeling hopeless, what does David declare in Psalm 89:52 (or verse 53)?

8. How does Jesus meet specific needs and give people hope in Sunday's gospel?
   Mark 1:29-31
   Mark 1:32-34
   Mark 1:38-39

9. How is Jesus strengthened to carry on meeting the needs of people and giving hope in Mark 1:35?

10. What do Simon and his companions do in Mark 1:36?

11. What universal truth for all people is expressed in Mark 1:37?

Reflection

1. At this point in Job's life, he sees life as drudgery, labouring day by day to exist. Life is misery. He is wishing his life away, hopeless, and convinced he will never see happiness. Can you relate to any of these feelings now or at some time in the past? Explain. How did you experience hope, or peace, or relief during a hard time?

2. Jesus brings healing in body and spirit and proclaims the good news. How can you help others find physical, emotional, and spiritual relief through Jesus?

3. How have you ever experienced burnout when serving and ministering to others? How do you seek strength for continued service?

4. Simon and his companions seek Jesus and proclaim, "Everyone is looking for you"? How do you seek Jesus? Our hearts were created to be restless until we rest in Jesus, even when we do not recognize our need. How does knowing this help you to be more willing to proclaim the good news?

Optional Exercise. Have each person in the group briefly share about an event from his or her past week or about an upcoming event. This could be a time to share a triumph, trial, or need.

Second Reading

1 Corinthians 9:16-19, 22-23

Setting the Stage

The next reading is from the first letter St. Paul writes to the church in Corinth, Greece, about A.D. 55. Paul is a tentmaker by trade before he is called by Jesus to be His apostle. He continues that trade while he preaches to avoid the criticism that he is "out for money." Do we put money above people?

Read the second reading. Reread this Scripture. What word, phrase, or idea stands out for you?

Exploring Further

1. How does Paul describe his duty to preach in 1 Corinthians 9:16?

2. How is Paul commissioned to preach the good news?
   Acts 9:11-19
   Acts 26:12-18

3. What does Paul freely give according to 1 Corinthians 9:18?

   Note: Paul is criticized for not accepting monetary support from the community or servants like the other apostles. Paul does not exercise this right because he is compelled to preach the gospel as a duty to God. He must fulfill this duty by proclaiming the gospel free of charge and with mercy, as God did to him.

4. What approach does Paul use in dealing with people according to 1 Corinthians 9:19-22?

5. How does Paul please both Jew and Gentiles in the following Scriptures?
   Acts 21:18-24
   Acts 21:25-26

6. Why does Paul give his life for the gospel according to 1 Corinthians 9:23?

Reflection

1. Have you ever felt compelled to do something because of your convictions, as a result of prayer, or as a duty laid on you by God? Explain.

2. Paul identified with those outside the law, those under the law, and the weak. He became like those with whom he shared the gospel. How can you identify with the destitute, the single parent, the gay community, different racial groups, the lonely, and other marginalized people in order to proclaim the gospel? What attitudes and prejudices would be an obstacle between these groups and you? What work would God need to do in you in order for you to proclaim the gospel with love?

Closing Prayer

Lord, help us to understand what it means to be Your people and to proclaim Your gospel. Give us Your love for all people. Amen.

Sixth Sunday of Ordinary Time
Year B

Opening Song

Opening Prayer

Open in prayer and invite everyone to add his or her own prayer. Close together: Lord, You forgive our transgressions and cover our sin. Touch us with Your love and mercy that we will be healed. Amen.

Review Study Guidelines

First Reading

Leviticus 13:1-2, 45-46

Setting the Stage

The first reading is from the book of Leviticus written in 1300. B.C. In it we see Moses and his brother, Aaron, leading the Hebrew people who are to follow certain rules and laws of conduct in their dealings with each other. We hear how persons with leprosy are supposed to act. Leprosy is the name given to all kinds of skin diseases, like rashes, eczema, etc. All who have it have to stay outside the camp until they are clean. Imagine how they must feel. In much the same manner, how do we feel when we are cut off from people?

Read the first reading aloud. Reread this Scripture. What word, phrase, or idea stands out for you?

Exploring Further

1. What action is required when a skin sore develops according to Leviticus 13:1-3?

2. How is the one with leprosy to act according to Leviticus 13:45-46?

3. What does Moses' sister Miriam do in Numbers 12:1-2?

4. What is the consequence in Numbers 12:9-15?

   Note: "White leprosy" is a skin disease that generally is not serious or of long duration.[33]

5. How do the Hebrew people remember this incident and what does it cause them to do in Deuteronomy 24:8-9?

6. How is someone who has leprosy restored to the community?
   Leviticus 14:2-10
   Leviticus 14:21-32

7. There are two instances in the Old Testament when God heals a leper. One is Miriam, which we read. Describe what happened the other time in 2 Kings 5:1, 9-14

8. How does Jesus respond to the leper in Sunday's gospel, Mark 1:40-42?

9. What does Jesus tell the healed leper to do in Mark 1:43-44?

10. What does the man do and what results according to Mark 1:45?

Reflection

1. At the time of Leviticus, why would a contagious disease be a grave concern?
   What diseases today cause fear and concern? Explain.

2. What groups of people are at risk of being treated as "lepers" today? In what way do we drive them from our communities? What or whom decides their return?

3. How is sin like a spiritual leprosy? How does sin exclude us from family, community, and life? How can we be purified to return?

Optional Exercise. Have each person in the group briefly share about an event from his or her past week or about an upcoming event. This could be a time to share a triumph, trial, or need.

Second Reading

1 Corinthians 10:23-11:1

Setting the Stage

The next reading is from St. Paul's first letter to the church in Corinth, Greece. He writes this from Ephesus (modern-day southwestern Turkey) about 25 years after the resurrection of Jesus. He is responding to questions and difficulties of the Corinthians. People are wondering if they can eat meat that has been used in pagan worship and sold in the meat markets. God our Father uses this question to teach us how we can help our neighbour who may have a tender conscience.

Read the second reading aloud. Reread this Scripture. What word, phrase, or idea stands out for you?

Exploring Further

1. What important qualifications to our liberty in Christ does Paul point out in 1 Corinthians 10:23-24?

2. What directions and reasoning does Paul give regarding eating meat that has been sacrificed to idols, either purchased from the market or offered in an unbelievers' home, in 1 Corinthians 10:25-27?

3. What principle does Paul base these statements on in 1 Corinthians 8:4-6?

4. What situation changes and what does Paul advise in 1 Corinthians 10:28-31?

5. What does Jesus say regarding food in Mark 7:14-15, 18-19?

6. What should our goal be in response to various situations?
   Romans 14:13-20
   Romans 15:1-4
   Philippians 2:3-8

7. How can we use our freedom responsibly according to 1 Corinthians 10:31-11:1?

8. What specific things mentioned in the following Scriptures should we imitated?
   Ephesians 4:31-5:2
   Hebrews 6:11-12

Reflection

1. What are examples of things that are lawful, but not beneficial or up-building?

2. Who is influenced by your good and bad examples?

3. In the above Scriptures some of the following principles are listed: pursue peace; mutual up-building; be steadfast; be encouraged by the Scriptures; regard others as better than self; look to the interest of others; be like Christ emptying self for us; humility and obedience; put up with failings of the weak; do not be selfish or conceited; forgive; give no offence; put aside bitterness, wrangling, and malice; be

kind, tender-hearted, a fragrant offering; and receive the Word with joy. Which of these do you find helpful in guiding your behaviour? Which of these do you struggle with? Who has been an example to you in some of these areas?

Closing Prayer

Lord, help us to be imitators of You that many will be drawn to Your love and You may be glorified. Amen.

Seventh Sunday of Ordinary Time
Year B

Opening Song

Opening Prayer

Open in prayer and invite everyone to add his or her own prayer. Close together: Lord, You have called us to be Your people, to sing Your praises. Blessed be God forever. Amen.

Review Study Guidelines

First Reading

Isaiah 43:18-22, 24-25

Setting the Stage

The first reading is from the book of the prophet Isaiah. These words of consolation are spoken as the Hebrew people are being allowed to return to Palestine in 538 B.C. They are like their ancestors of old who went over desert roads to find freedom after escaping from slavery in Egypt. Note the two names "Jacob" and "Israel." They are the two names given first to the grandson of Abraham, and then later given to the entire Hebrew nation. They have become our names too! In spite of our sins, what can we expect from God our Father?

Read the first reading aloud. Reread this Scripture. What word, phrase, or idea stands out for you?

Exploring Further

1. What work of God is remembered in Isaiah 43:16-17?

2. What does God promise to do in Isaiah 43:18-19?

3. What does God promise to do?
   Isaiah 65:17-18
   Revelation 21:3-5

4. How is God's coming described in Isaiah 35:3-6?

5. How is Jesus' coming described and what new thing is He doing in Sunday's gospel, Mark 2:1-5?

6. Why is God forming a people?
   Isaiah 43:20-21
   1 Peter 2:9-10

7. How do we become part of this people according to 2 Corinthians 5:17-18?

8. What have God's people failed to do in Isaiah 43:22-23?

9. What wearies God according to Isaiah 43:24?

10. How do the teachers of the law weary Jesus in Sunday's gospel Mark 2:6-8?

11. In spite of our sin, what does God do and why according to Isaiah 43:25?

12. How does Jesus show mercy in Mark 2:9-11?

13. How do the people respond in Mark 2:12?

Reflection

1. In Isaiah the new thing God is doing is compared to water in the wilderness or rivers in a desert. What new, refreshing, or life-giving thing is God doing in you?

2. God is forming a people who will announce His praises. What have you witnessed or experienced so as to proclaim God's praises?

3. Do you tend to call on God quickly or as a last resort? Explain. How do you offer worship and sacrifice to God?

4. Though God forgives and forgets, how might Isaiah 43:25 be helpful if you are having trouble forgiving yourself? Though we do not want to dwell on past sins, why is it helpful to remember the mercy, healing, and wisdom we received from God? What does God's mercy mean to you?

Optional Exercise. Have each person in the group briefly share about an event from his or her past week or about an upcoming event. This could be a time to share a triumph, trial, or need.

Second Reading

2 Corinthians 1:18-22

Setting the Stage

The next reading is from the second letter St. Paul wrote to the church in Corinth, Greece, about 25 years after the resurrection of Jesus. Paul, along with his friends Silvanus and Timothy, has brought the good news of Jesus there. But the Corinthians are making accusations against Paul; they say he cannot keep his word because he has not kept an appointment to visit them earlier. In response, Paul compares himself to Jesus. Note the Hebrew word that we use often, "Amen." It means "Yes." Do we see ourselves saying yes to God our Father through Jesus when we come to Mass?

Read the second reading aloud. Reread this Scripture. What word, phrase, or idea stands out for you?

Exploring Further

1. The Corinthians are upset and doubting Paul's integrity. How does Paul explain his change of plans and defend himself in 2 Corinthians 1:12, 15-17?

2. Despite Paul appearing unfaithful because of his change of plans, what truth does he reaffirm?
   2 Corinthians 1:18
   1 Corinthians 1:9

3. What does Jesus say about promises in Matthew 5:33 and 37?

4. What is God's yes to us according to 2 Corinthians 1:19-20?

5. What four things does God do for us according to 2 Corinthians 1:21-22?

6. What are we given to confirm God's yes in Jesus?
   Romans 5:5, 6:4
   1 Corinthians 1:5-7
   Ephesians 1:13-14
   1 John 2:20

Reflection

1. The Corinthians were upset over Paul's change of plans. How flexible are you when plans change and how do you deal with the disappointment? Have you ever changed plans when others where counting

on you? Can you say, as Paul did, that your change of plans was God directed? Can you trust God when plans change?

2. When have you experienced God's faithfulness in the past? In what situation do you presently trust God to be faithful?

3. The above Scriptures tell us that in Jesus we are marked and sealed, given spiritual gifts, anointed; know truth, are buried with Him in baptism to rise with Him at the resurrection, and we received the Holy Spirit. We are God's possession and the Holy Spirit is a down payment on our eternal inheritance. Describe the security that this gives you. What evidence is there in your life that you believe these truths? Explain.

Closing Prayer

I will tell of Your marvelous works. I will rejoice and be glad in You, and sing to Your name Most High. Amen. (Psalm 9:1-2)

Eighth Sunday of Ordinary Time
Year B

Opening Song

Opening Prayer

Open in prayer and invite everyone to add his or her own prayer. Close together: Lord, You are kind and merciful, forgiving our iniquities, healing our diseases, and redeeming our lives. Amen.

Review Study Guidelines

First Reading

Hosea 2:14-15 (or 16-17) 19-20 (or 21-22)
The numbering in Hosea varies in different translations. This study is based on the NRSV.

Setting the Stage

The first reading is from the book of prophet Hosea. Hosea lives in the northern kingdom, Israel, about 750 years before Jesus. Hosea's own troubled marriage becomes a touching symbol of God our Father's relationship with His Hebrew people. They have deserted Him by not practicing their religion sincerely. Even though they are unfaithful, we hear God our Father's reaction. When we have sinned, are we able to hear these words?

Read the first reading aloud. This reading starts with "I will allure her and bring her into the wilderness." Reread this Scripture. What word, phrase, or idea stands out for you?

Exploring Further

1. Where will God lead his people and why according to Hosea 2:14-15 (or verse 16-17)?

2. What does going to the desert recall for the Israelites in Exodus 13:17-18a, 20-22?

   Note: This, properly speaking, is the beginning of the exodus, the journey of God's people through the desert to the Promised Land; the prophets were to look back on this time as the first days of God's marriage to his people.[34] For Hosea, as for Amos, the desert life of the Exodus represents a lost ideal; Israel was still a child, knew nothing about foreign gods, and followed Yahweh faithfully.[35]

3. How is Israel's relationship to God described?
   Hosea 2:16
   Hosea 11:1, 3-4
   Jeremiah 2:2-3

4. The "Valley or Achor" is referred to in Hosea 2:15 (or 17). What happened here according to Joshua 7:20-25?

5. How will God use this valley now?
   Hosea 2:15
   Isaiah 65:10

6. What does God promise in Hosea 2:19-20 (or verse 21-22)?

7. How is the relationship with God and his people described?
   Isaiah 62:5
   Mark 2:18-20, Sunday's gospel
   Revelation 21:2-3

8. How do people who "know God's love" respond to God?
   Hosea 6:6
   Psalm 1:1-2
   Psalm 43:4

9. Hosea portrays God wanting to take us, the beloved, to a desert place where we are not distracted and must rely on Him. God desires we be attentive and trusting. He will love us as a husband. God will pour His love and His Spirit into our hearts. What condition must our hearts be in to receive this love according to the analogy Jesus uses in Mark 2:21-22, Sunday's gospel?

   Note: A wineskin was a goatskin sewn together at the edges to form a watertight bag. New wine, expanding as it aged, stretched the wineskin. New wine, therefore, could not be put into a wineskin that had already been stretched or the taut skin would burst…Your heart, like a wineskin, can become rigid and prevent you from accepting the new life that Christ offers. Keep your heart pliable and open to accepting the life-changing truths of Jesus' message.[36]

Reflection

1. What distractions in your life keep you from hearing and/or trusting God? What "desert" experiences brought you to a place of listening to and reliance on God?

2. Lent is a time to retreat to a "desert" place (less distractions and more simplicity) to listen and spend time with God. Here we can reflect on God's tender words of reproach and encouragement and reevaluate our lives. How might you take steps to meet God in this "desert" place this Lent?

3. Marriage is often used to express God's relationship with His people. Comparing your relationship with God to a marriage, how well are you getting along with Him right now? Are you married singles? Good friends? On a honeymoon? Divorced? Comfortable together? Have a rock-solid marriage? Giving each other the silent treatment? Other? What is your reaction to the idea that God is your husband or Jesus is your bridegroom?

Optional Exercise. Have each person in the group briefly share about an event from his or her past week or about an upcoming event. This could be a time to share a triumph, trial, or need.

Second Reading

2 Corinthians 3:1-6

Setting the Stage

The next reading is from the second letter St. Paul writes to the church in Corinth, Greece. Paul has set up this church around the year 50 A.D., but he does not have any written credentials. Some of his opponents came along later and told the Christians not to trust Paul because of that, and they say he is not preaching the truth. In a play on words, Paul compares the way the letters of the Ten Commandments are written to the way the Holy Spirit now writes. Through these words, God our Father tells us which *way* is more important.

Read the second reading aloud. Reread this Scripture. What word, phrase, or idea stands out for you?

Exploring Further

1. Paul is again under attack from his opponents, this time for not having written credentials. What is Paul's response in 2 Corinthians 3:1-2 and 10:18?

2. What comparisons does Paul make in 2 Corinthians 3:3?

3. How is this comparison a fulfillment of what was prophesied?
   Jeremiah 31:33
   Ezekiel 11:19

4. What do we receive through Jesus Christ according to 2 Corinthians 3:4?

5. Who does Paul give credit to and for what in 2 Corinthians 3:5?

6. Why can we not take credit for any ministry?
    John 3:27
    Ephesians 3:7

7. Having received the Holy Spirit, how are we to live according to Colossians 1:22-23?

8. What comparison is made between the law and the Spirit in 2 Corinthians 3:6?

9. What is the law that is referred to in Exodus 24:12?

10. What is the purpose of the law according to Romans 7:7-8, 12-13?

    Note: The purpose of the law is to define sin and make people conscious of their sin, but it does not provide spiritual strength. Through the promised Spirit we are given inward life and strength to do all good things.

Reflection

1. Have you ever considered yourself a letter of Christ's? What kind of letter are you? An encouraging letter? A good news letter? A love letter? Or are you hard to read? Confusing and inconsistent? Other?

2. How have you delivered or helped deliver letters for Christ? Who has been a letter of Christ for you?

3. How can you relate to the difference between trying to follow "the letter of the law" to become good or to earn God's love as opposed to receiving the life of the Spirit? How has experiencing the Holy Spirit helped?

Closing Prayer

God of salvation, empower us to be letters of Christ for all to read. Amen.

Ninth Sunday of Ordinary Time
Year B

Opening Song

Opening Prayer

Open in prayer and invite everyone to add his or her prayer. Close together: Lord, teach us what it means to keep Your Sabbath day holy. Amen.

Review Study Guidelines

First Reading

Deuteronomy 5:12-15

Setting the Stage

The first reading is from the book of Deuteronomy. "Deuteronomy" is a Greek word meaning "the second law." It takes the Law of Moses written in the book of Exodus and explains it in everyday language.[37] We hear about the rule of keeping the Sabbath.[38] "Sabbath" is a Hebrew word whose root means "to cease work," "to rest." To us moderns who are workaholics and busy weekenders, God our Father gives an important reminder.

Read the first reading aloud. Reread this Scripture. What word, phrase, or idea stands out for you?

Exploring Further

1. What are we commanded to do in Deuteronomy 5:12?

2. What are we to cease from doing according to Deuteronomy 5:13-14?

3. What reason is given for this in Exodus 20:11?

4. How did the Israelites live this out in the desert according to Exodus 16:21-28?

5. Who is specifically included in the command to cease from work that might otherwise have been overlooked in Deuteronomy 5:14?

6. What reason is given for including slaves and foreigners?
    Deuteronomy 5:15
    Deuteronomy 15:12-15

7. What does Jesus do on the Sabbath and what is his explanation in Sunday's gospel, Mark 2:23-26?

8. What does David do according to 1 Samuel 21:1-6?

9. What is the law regarding the temple bread according to Leviticus 24:5-9?

10. What is the higher law in Sunday's gospel, Mark 2:27-28?

11. How is the difference between the spirit of the law and the letter of the law?
    Luke 6:6-11
    2 Corinthians 3:6

12. What results when we honour the Sabbath according to Isaiah 58:13-14?

Reflection

1. In our period of history, Sundays have become like any other day. How does this affect families, single parents, low income workers, executives in demanding jobs, relationships, stress levels, efficiency, and other areas of life?

2. One Sabbath extreme is "business as usual" and another extreme is a legalistic attitude where Sabbath rest is used for selfish means rather than to help others. What are some examples of these two attitudes in our world today?

3. "Sunday worship fulfills the moral command of the Old covenant, taking up its rhythm and spirit in the weekly celebration of the Creator and Redeemer of his people."[39] In today's reading we hear of the people's obligation regarding the Sabbath. How is the obligation to attend Sunday Eucharist similar? Why is Sunday worship still a grave obligation for us? Is Sunday worship a burden for you or a time of delight in the Lord?

Optional Exercise. Have each person in the group briefly share about an event from his or her past week or about an upcoming event. This could be a time to share a triumph, trial, or need.

Second Reading

2 Corinthians 4:6-11

Setting the Stage

The next reading is from the second letter St. Paul writes about 25 years after the resurrection of Jesus to the church in Corinth, Greece. The Corinthians have begun to lose trust in Paul; some accuse him of not teaching clearly[40] and of keeping them in the dark. In response, Paul tells them frankly and openly what it is like for him to be a priest carrying the good news of Jesus. As we face similar criticism when carrying the same message to people, how are we supposed to handle it?

Read the second reading aloud. Reread this Scripture. What word, phrase, or idea stands out for you?

Exploring Further

1. What light shines in our hearts according to 2 Corinthians 4:6?

2. When and how does light come to be in Genesis 1:1-4?

3. Just as the sun lights people on their way, so anything that shows them the way to God is "light."[41]
    What is light in the following Scriptures?
    Psalm 119:105
    Matthew 5:14-16
    John 8:12

4. What do light and darkness symbolize in the following Scriptures?
    John 3:19-21
    Romans 13:11-13
    Colossians 1:12-13
    Revelation 22:5

5. Who does God entrust with the message of light and salvation in 2 Corinthians 4:7?

6. Why does he entrust this message to such frail vessels according to the following?
    2 Corinthians 4:7
    1 Corinthians 1:26-31
    Judges 7:2-7
    1 Samuel 17:47, 50

7. What can we expect when we are vessels for the light and glory of Christ?
   2 Corinthians 4:8-9
   1 Corinthians 4:11-13

8. When we suffer for the sake of the kingdom, what do we share in and who benefits?
   2 Corinthians 4:10-12
   Philippians 3:8-11
   Colossians 1:24-27

Reflection

1. Scripture, Jesus, and fellow believers are three ways the light of Christ is revealed. Which of these ways did God use to give revelation in your life?

2. In Scripture, light symbolizes truth, salvation, protection, kingdom, life, and walking in the ways of Christ. Darkness symbolizes evil, sinful acts, being under the power of evil, and separation from Christ. How have you experienced the kingdom of light and the kingdom of darkness? How did you move out of darkness into light?

3. How has being a vessel for God brought suffering, persecution, or hardship to you?

4. "Suffering, a consequence of original sin, acquires a new meaning; it becomes a participation in the saving work of Jesus."[42] There is also an old saying that the blood of martyrs is the seed bed of faith. Where have you seen, experienced, or read about suffering that resulted in life and healing?

Closing Prayer

Lord, through our suffering, may many come to life. Help us to always know that we can do all things through Him who strengthens us. Amen.

SECTION FOUR

LENT

Lent is a period of forty days of preparation and does not include Sundays, which are always celebrated as "mini Easters."

In the time of Noah, it rained for forty days and forty nights, destroying the old way of life and preparing Noah for a new life. Moses and the Israelites spent forty years in the desert learning to know and trust God, their redeemer. Jesus spent forty days in the desert, totally trusting God in preparation for his ministry.

The traditional hallmarks of Lent are prayer, fasting, and almsgiving.

Jesus' time of prayer in the desert before embarking on his ministry is intense. What does this say to you about your need to set aside a time for more intense prayer? Lent is such a time.

Jesus' fasts in the desert make him weak and vulnerable. In doing so, he experiences strength by trusting God. By emptying himself, Jesus is able to be filled with the Spirit and power of God. Self-reliance prevents God-reliance. What do you need to fast from in order to be vulnerable and to rely on God? Is your life so full that you have failed to leave room for God or the things of God? What do you need to empty from your life to make room for God?

We are called to give alms, to be aware of those in need and to help them. We need to be generous because God is generous to us. When we give generously of ourselves, we deepen our trust in God's care and providence for us.

> Is not this the fast that I choose: to loose the bonds of injustice, to undo the thongs of the yoke, to let the oppressed go free, and to break every yoke? Is it not to share your bread with the hungry, and bring the homeless poor into your house; when you see the naked, to cover them, and not to hide yourself from your own kin?
>
> —Isaiah 58:6-7

Prayer, fasting, and almsgiving are always connected with justice. As we seek a deeper relationship with Jesus, we will be led to seek just relationships with and for others.

Lord, help me to use these forty days of Lent to let go of the old life and be open to the new life you have for me. Help me to become empty and vulnerable so that I may be filled with you. Teach me to trust you and to give generously of my time, resources, and talents just as you give so generously to me. Lord, show me where my life contributes to injustice for others and give me the courage to change. Help me use these forty days wisely. Amen.

The wages of sin is death,
but the free gift of God is
eternal life
in Christ Jesus our Lord.

(Romans 6:23)

FIRST SUNDAY OF LENT
YEAR B

Opening Song

Opening Prayer

Open in prayer and invite everyone to add his or her own prayer. Close together: Lord, You are merciful and faithful to the people You have called by name and made Your own. Help us be faithful to Your commandments, that we may have life. Amen.

Review Study Guidelines

First Reading

Genesis 9:8-15

Setting the Stage

During Lent there are special readings in preparation for Easter. Today, God our Father speaks to us about water in all three readings because during Lent we are preparing to renew our baptism. The first reading is from the book of Genesis. We hear the story of Noah and his ark. This story is used by God to teach us the answers to these questions:

1. What can we expect from God after baptism?
2. What are we to think of when we look at a rainbow in the sky?

Read the first reading aloud. Reread this Scripture. What word, phrase, or idea stands out for you?

Exploring Further

1. What is the covenant God makes in Genesis 9:11?

2. Who is this covenant with according to Genesis 9:12?

3. What is the sign of this covenant In Genesis 9:13?

    Note: You'll find *covenant* is a theme woven throughout Scripture. Scripture reveals how God has used covenants to forge family bonds with people of every age. The basic message God wants to convey by a covenant, then, can be stated simply: "I love you. I am committed to you. I swear that I will never forsake you. You are mine and I am yours. I am your Father and you are my family." How astonishing that the Creator has such profound Love for His creatures![43] Each covenant is God initiated. Each further develops and expands God's family. In each, God swears a promise to His people that He is faithful too.

    ## Our Family Tree of Covenants at a Glance[44]

Covenant Mediator	Adam	Noah	Abram	Moses	David	Jesus
Covenant Role	Husband	Father	Chieftain	Judge	King	Royal High Priest
Covenant Form	Marriage	Household	Tribe	Nation	National Kingdom	Universal Family
Sign	Sabbath	Rainbow	Circumcision	Passover	Throne	Eucharist

4. What is the covenant God made and with whom in Genesis 17:4-7?

5. What is the sign of this covenant according to Genesis 17:11?

6. Name the covenant and its sign found in Matthew 26:28?

7. How do we enter this covenant according to Romans 6:3-4?

    Just as a common name unites a family, we as the Church are united through baptism, rebirth and adoption into God's family in the name of the Father, Son, and Holy Spirit. The sacramental bond of baptism reflects a covenant oath which Christ has established…And this bond is perfected and strengthened when we received the flesh and blood of the Father's firstborn Son, the Passover Lamb of the New Covenant, in the power of the Spirit.[45]

8. What does Jesus proclaim and what are we called to do in Sunday's gospel, Mark 1:14-15?

Reflection

1. In the first reading, God makes a covenant with "all living things." With this in mind, how can you show care and respect for creation?

2. What does this covenant imply in regard to our responsibility to life at all stages? How can you celebrate or affirm someone's life this week, maybe your own!?

3. The rainbow is a sign that God is faithful to His promise. Where in your life do you desire a promise from God? Or where in your life has God given you a promise you are trusting?

4. If your group leader were to hand you a check for one million dollars, you would probably throw it in the trash knowing it would bounce. If you looked more closely and the check was cosigned by the government of your country as the guarantor, you would probably head straight for the bank. Our heavenly Father is the guarantor of all the promises and covenants made in Scripture. To what degree do you live your life as if you really believe God's promises?

Optional Exercise. Have each person in the group briefly share about an event from his or her past week or about an upcoming event. This could be a time to share a triumph, trial, or need.

Second Reading

1 Peter 3:18-22

Setting the Stage

This reading is from the first letter of Peter written in about the year A.D. 64 to Christians in Asia (modern-day western Turkey). They are suffering persecution from unbelieving neighbours. This symbolic language expresses the fact that Jesus, by His death and resurrection, has conquered all evil and suffering. What do baptized believers do when in tough times? Who do we turn to?

Read the second reading aloud. Reread this Scripture. What word, phrase, or idea stands out for you?

Exploring Further

1. Why and for whom does Christ die for according to 1 Peter 3:18?

2. According to the following Scriptures and the quotes from the catechism, who is reached and affected by the power of Christ's death and resurrection?
   1 Peter 3:19-20a
   1 Peter 4:5-6

   CCB 632: The frequent New Testament affirmations that Jesus was "raised from the dead" presuppose that the crucified one sojourned in the realm of the dead prior to his resurrection. This was the first meaning given to the apostolic preaching to Christ's descent into hell: that Jesus, like all men, experienced death and in his soul joined the others in the realm of the dead. But he descended there as Saviour, proclaiming the good news to the spirits imprisoned there.[46]

   CCB 634: "The gospel was preached even to the dead." The descent into hell brings the Gospel message of salvation to complete fulfillment. This is the last phase of Jesus' messianic mission, a phase which is condensed in time but vast in its real significance: the spread of Christ's redemptive work to all people of all times and all places, for all who are saved have been made sharers in the redemption.[47]

3. What prefigures baptism according to 1 Peter 3:20b?

4. What virtue of God is mentioned in the following Scriptures?
    1 Peter 3:20
    2 Peter 3:9

5. What saves us and how according to 1 Peter 3:21?

6. How does Jesus suffer after His baptism and who attends to Him in Sunday's gospel, Mark 1:12-13?

7. Christ suffered for us. What hope do we have in times of suffering in Romans 8:35-39?

8. Where does Christ now reside and in what position of authority according to 1 Peter 3:22?

Reflection

1. In the above Scriptures, we read that Jesus died for sinners, preached the good news to the dead, and nothing can come between us and God's love poured out in Christ Jesus. How does this give you hope for hopeless situations in your life? For loved ones who seem "dead" to the good news? For barriers or walls that seem to stand between you and God?

2. When did God break through barriers such as fear, pain, loneliness, hopelessness, etc., and bring you life, love, or good news? Explain.

3. Every Easter we renew the promise we made at baptism which is: "Do you reject Satan? And all his works? And all his empty promises?" Then we renew our statement of faith. Through baptism, what does God do for us and what is our part in this covenant?

4. Would you consider yourself patient or impatient with other people when they are slow or make mistakes or do things differently than you? What is one way God has shown patience with you on your faith journey? How might you prepare so as to respond patiently the next time your patience is tested?

Closing Prayer

Father, through our observance of Lent, teach us Your ways and lead us on Your path of truth. Grant us the grace to repent and believe the good news. Amen.

Second Sunday of Lent
Year B

Opening Song

Opening Prayer

Open in prayer and invite everyone to add his or her own prayer. Close together: Speak, Lord; I am listening. Plant Your Word down deep inside me. Amen.

Review Study Guidelines

First Reading

Genesis 22:1-2, 9-13, 15-18

Setting the Stage

The first reading is from the book of Genesis. We hear of a special event in the life of Abraham, about 1800 years before Jesus. The pagan peoples living in Palestine at this time have the terrible false and cruel idea that their gods want them to offer their children in sacrifice. It is strange and shocking to hear that Abraham is being asked to do the same. In the end, however, we hear God our Father stopping Abraham from doing this. It's important to focus on Abraham's intention: What is in his heart that makes him acceptable and pleasing to God our Father?

Read the first reading aloud. Reread this Scripture. What word, phrase, or idea stands out for you?

Exploring Further

1. How does Abraham answer when God calls him in Genesis 22:1?

2. Where does Abraham take Isaac and what is the test according to Genesis 22:2?

3. Where does Jesus take his disciples in Sunday's gospel and who greets them in Mark 9:2-4?

4. What are some reasons God tests our faith?
   Exodus 16:4
   Deuteronomy 8:2
   James 1:2-4

5. Abraham's faith and obedience is remembered even today. What do the following Scriptures emphasize regarding faith and obedience?
   Galatians 5:5-6
   James 2:20-26
   1 John 2:3-6

6. What questions does Isaac have in Genesis 22:7?

7. What questions do the disciples have in Sunday gospel Mark 9:9-10?

8. How does Isaac display trust in Genesis 22:8-9?

9. How does Isaac foreshadow Jesus in John 19:17

10. How does God intervene in Genesis 22:10-12?

11. How does Abraham's test foreshadow the sacrifice of God the Father in John 3:16?

12. How does God affirm His love for His only son in Mark 9:5-8, Sunday's gospel?

13. What does God provide in Genesis 22:13-14?

14. What does God provide in John 1:29?

Reflection

1. When God calls, Abraham's response is, "Here I am," or, "Ready." Does this availability reflect your response to God? Explain? How does God call us today?

2. Isaac trusts his father even though he does not understand. When have you chosen to trust or cling to God in the face of uncertain or unknown circumstances? What was the result?

3. Abraham is obedient and stands firm in his faith in God even when it appears to be leading to the death of his future hopes and dreams. When have you let go of your agenda or plans and acted in obedience to God, spouse, employer, etc., even when it felt like part of you (maybe pride or hope) was dying? What was the result?

4. Are you afraid of what God may ask of you? Explain. Which of the following do you entrust to God's care and where do you struggle to trust: your spouse, children; health, career; possessions, retirement, money, death?

5. What are the benefits of having your faith tested and when have you received benefits from the testing of your faith?

Optional Exercise. Have each person in the group briefly share about an event from his or her past week or about an upcoming event. This could be a time to share a triumph, trial, or need.

Second Reading

Romans 8:31b-35, 37

Setting the Stage

The next reading is from the letter of St. Paul written to the church in Rome about 27 years after the resurrection of Jesus. Today's reading is the end of chapter 8, which lists what God our Father has done for us. In fact, He has done so much that we can ask ourselves if anything can stop the love of God from getting through to us.

Read the second reading aloud. Reread this Scripture. What word, phrase, or idea stands out for you?

Exploring Further

1. What is the great act of love mentioned in the following Scriptures?
   Roman 8:31-32
   Romans 5:6-8

2. What does God do for us according to the following Scriptures?
   Romans 8:28
   Romans 8:33
   Romans 8:34

3. What is our hope in hardship and suffering in Romans 8:35-39?

4. What is the fruit of suffering and hardship?
   Romans 5:3-5
   2 Corinthians 4:7-10

5. What do we conquer hardship with according to 1 John 5:3-5?

Reflection

1. What have you learned or how have you matured through suffering? How did suffering change or shape your relationship with God?

2. How were you supported and loved during a hard time? Explain. What did people do that was helpful? What would you recommend people *not do* when they are attempting to help?

Closing Prayer

For I am certain that neither death nor life, neither angels nor principalities, neither the present nor the future, nor powers, neither height nor depth nor any other creature, will be able to separate us from the love of God that come to us in Christ Jesus, our Lord. Amen.

—Romans 8:38-39 NAS

Third Sunday of Lent
Year B

Note For parishes engaged in the Rite of Christian Initiation for Adults, this Sunday is the first scrutiny. The readings from third Sunday Year C-A, "Come and Drink," will be read.

Opening Song

Opening Prayer

Open in prayer and invite everyone to add his or her own prayer. Close together: Lord, Your words bring us to life. May we receive them and live them. Amen.

Review Study Guidelines

First Reading

Exodus 20:1-17

Setting the Stage

The first reading is from the book of Exodus. We hear about the journey of the Hebrew people from slavery in Egypt to freedom in Palestine around 1300 B.C., under the leadership of Moses. Today's reading gives us familiar words; they are the core, the central message that God our Father spoke when the Hebrews were at Mount Sinai. As we journey through Lent toward Easter, can we live these words more intensely?

Read the first reading aloud. Reread this Scripture. What word, phrase, or idea stands out for you?

Exploring Further

1. The first commandment calls us to fidelity. What is this commandment in Exodus 20:1-6?

2. How does God describe our turning away from Him through sin in Hosea 1:2, 3:1?

3. What do these Scriptures say about God's love, even when we are unfaithful?
   Hosea 2:14 (or verse 16)
   Hosea 2:19-20 (or verses 21-22)

4. How are we to honour God according to Exodus 20:7?

5. What do the following Scriptures make clear regarding the Sabbath?
   Exodus 20:8-11
   Exodus 31:12-17
   Exodus 34:21
   Hebrews 4:1-4

6. What insight does Jesus give regarding the Sabbath in Luke 13:14-17?

7. What is Jesus' response to the misuse of the temple in Sunday's gospel John 2:13-16?

8. What relationships and practice of respect are dealt with in the remaining seven commandments in Exodus 20:13-17?

9. How are these seven commandments summed up in Romans 13:8-10?

10. Paraphrase the Ten Commandments and personalize them with "I will" instead of "you shall not."

Reflection

1. To be faithful, one must first be in a personal two-way relationship. How can we enter a personal relationship with God and nurture this relationship? How does God enter into and nurture a relationship with us?

2. The Sabbath is a day to choose to trust God, to wait upon God, and to rest in God.

   The Sabbath was to be a day set aside to joyfully live out our dependence on God. As the psalm says, "This is the day that the Lord has made. Let us be glad and rejoice in it" (Psalm 118:21). The Sabbath rest is the Lord's way of teaching us that he is the real power in our lives. He says, in effect, "Just one day a week, stop achieving, stop accomplishing, stop doing anything that is task-oriented. On that day, let me do the achieving, let me do the saving." That is the real meaning of the third commandment: freedom from willfulness.[48]

   • How do we as a society reflect and honour Sabbath rest, trusting God to care for us?
   • Think of one or two ways you can start, or continue, to honour this commandment.

3. "The Tenth Commandment. I've never in all my years as a Catholic Christian heard a sermon on the tenth commandment. We can't possibly preach on "Thou shalt not covet thy neighbor's goods" because Western society is based on that. It's called capitalism. Mass advertising tells us we need things none of us need. It sows confusion about what's important for life. The level of need has moved to such a level of illusion and sophistication

that what were once ultimate luxuries have become necessities. In our culture, people cannot feel good about themselves unless next year's vacation is more luxurious than last year's, unless everything is upgraded—while most of God's people on this earth starve.

The affluent West has made happiness impossible. We've created pseudo-happiness, a pseudo-security that will never satisfy the human heart. Most of God's people are forced to learn to find happiness and freedom at a much more simple level. The gospel says that's where happiness is always to be found. That is about as traditional, old-fashioned, conservative a gospel as there is, and it will never change. We have to keep saying it: There is a Tenth commandment."[49]

- What factors in our daily lives increase our desire to have more material things?
- How can we reduce the influence of the above factors and be more discerning about defining genuine need versus excess?
- God's gifts are always to be used for the benefit of all. What goods have you been given? What are some ways you can use these for God's service?

Optional Exercise. Have each person in the group briefly share about an event from his or her past week or about an upcoming event. This could be a time to share a triumph, trial, or need.

Second Reading

1 Corinthians 1:18, 22-25

Setting the Stage
The second reading is from the first letter St. Paul wrote to the church in Corinth, Greece, about 25 years after the resurrection of Jesus. This church has division and disunity because some believe they are more intelligent and better educated than others. In response, Paul says, "Look at Jesus on the cross! How does that make sense?" Is human life always logical? Or is there mystery and paradox all around us?

Read the second reading aloud. Reread this Scripture. What word, phrase, or idea stands out for you?

Exploring Further

1. What are the two opposing ways of seeing the cross in 1 Corinthians 1:18?

2. What do the Jews demand in 1 Corinthians 1:22?

3. When asked for a sign, what response does Jesus give and what does it mean?
   Matthew 12:38-40
   John 2:18-22, Sunday's gospel

4. What sign is given in Sunday's gospel John 2:23-25?

5. What do the Greeks desire and what wisdom are they given in 1 Corinthians 1:22-24?

6. How can Jesus be both sanctuary and stumbling block?
   1 Corinthians 1:25
   1 Peter 2:6-8

   From the human point of view the cross goes against all expectations both of Jews and of Greeks; it is a rejection rather than a glorious manifestation, foolishness instead of wisdom. But to the eyes of faith the cross is the climax and overflow of the expectations, the power and wisdom of God.[50]

Reflection

1. Faith cannot be proven. To live in faith, which is to live in God, one has to risk looking foolish to some and being rejected by others. Can you think of a time when you were rejected or looked foolish because of your faith? Explain.

2. Was there a time in your life when you wanted proof that the Christian faith was true? Did you ever ridicule others for their faith? Explain.

3. Describe the faith experience you had when you first understood that God loved you, or had forgiven you, or was present at that moment, or that His Word was true?

Closing Prayer

Lord, through this examination of conscience, prepare our hearts to make a sincere confession this Lent. Thank You for being faithful and just, and when we do confess our sins, You cleanse us from all transgression. Amen.

An examination of conscience[51]
1. I am the Lord your God; you shall have no other gods before me.
   • Do I worship God in spirit and truth and give God the praise due Him?
   • Am I angry with God or resentful toward Him because of illness or other misfortunes?
   • Do I make a god out of my work, my possessions, or my image in the eyes of others so that these rule my life instead of God?
   • Have I tried to grow in the knowledge of God through prayer and Scripture reading?
   • Have I ever dabbled in occult or given credence to horoscopes, Ouija boards, channeling, tarot cards, or fortune-telling?
   • Have I taken time to teach my family about the ways of God and to pray with them?

2. You shall not take the name of the Lord, your God, in vain.
   • Have I been hypocritical by adhering to ritualistic observance while my heart has been far from God?
   • Have I resorted to profane language by cursing and swearing?

- In conversation, have I passively acceded to slander and jokes aimed at demeaning religion, the Church, or God's authority?

3. Remember the Sabbath day, and keep it holy.
   - Have I allowed myself to become so dominated by my work or chores that I have not set aside Sunday for spiritual and family activities?
   - Have I attended Mass every Sunday?
   - In my prayer and attendance at the liturgy, am I content with a passive observance rather than devoting myself to genuine worship of the Lord?

4. Honour your father and your mother.
   - As a young person in the family home, do I listen to, respect, and obey my parents?
   - As an adult, do I visit and care for my parents in their old age?
   - Do I harbour short-term or long-standing resentments toward my parents? Do I blame my parents for my own shortcomings?

5. You shall not kill.
   - Have I ever struck anyone in anger, intending to injure the person?
   - Have I ever had an abortion or advocated abortion or euthanasia, either through my opinions in conversation or by actively assisting someone?
   - Have I misused alcohol so that I later regretted my words, actions, or example?
   - Has my alcohol or drug abuse ever endangered my life or another person's life?

6. You shall not commit adultery.
   - Have I engaged in sexual activity outside of marriage?
   - Have I been involved in a homosexual relationship?
   - Have I given my mind over to lustful thoughts or fantasies?
   - Have I read pornography or watched indecent movies or television shows?
   - In conversation, have I told or enjoyed lewd or obscene jokes or stories?
   - Have I devalued my spouse through word or action?

7. You shall not steal.
   - Have I taken anything that did not belong to me?
   - Have I been dishonest in the payment of my taxes or in the submission of expense accounts in my business?
   - Have I wasted time and cheated my employer by not doing a full day's work?
   - Have I been extravagant in my manner of life, to the neglect of the poor?
   - Have I been irresponsible and neglected the needs of my family by wasting money on gambling or betting?

8. You shall not bear false witness against your neighbor.
   - Have I defamed the good name of another person by taking part in gossip or slander?
   - Have I injured the reputation of others by speaking about their failures and sins?
   - Have I condoned prejudice and hatred toward people of other nationalities, races, or religions?

9. You shall not covet your neighbor's wife.
   - Have I sought the affections of another's spouse?
   - Have I upheld the dignity of my spouse in all circumstances?
   - Have I rejected my family in my heart, wishing to distance myself emotionally and personally from them?

10. You shall not covet your neighbor's goods.
    - Do I have and express concern for those who are suffering, by giving generously to the poor or by serving those in need?
    - Do I habitually compare myself with others in terms of wealth, status, and financial security?
    - Am I jealous of the personal qualities of others or envious of their possessions or success?
    - Do I keep my finances in order and exercise proper stewardship over what is mine?
    - Do I support my church sufficiently?

Fourth Sunday of Lent
Year B

Note For parishes engaged in the RCIA, this Sunday is the second scrutiny. The readings from the fourth Sunday of Lent year C-A, "Come and Drink," will be read.

Opening Song

Opening Prayer

Open in prayer and invite everyone to add his or her own prayer. Close together: Lord Jesus Christ, Son of the living God, have mercy on us. Amen.

Review Study Guidelines

First Reading

2 Chronicles 36:14-17, 19-23

Setting the Stage
The first reading is from the second book of Chronicles. We hear the last verses of this book, which describe the terrible disaster that takes place in 587 B.C. Jerusalem and the temple, which are built on the hill called Zion, are destroyed and many Hebrew people are deported by the Babylonians, also known as the "Chaldeans." The Psalm following this reading describes the grief of the deported Hebrews. We hear what happens to them after the Babylonians are defeated in 539 B.C. by the Persian King, Cyrus the Second. Note the expression "the wrath of the Lord." By these words, the Hebrew people describe the consequences of their sin. Do we suffer the consequences of our sins?

Read the first reading aloud. Reread this Scripture. What word, phrase, or idea stands out for you?

Exploring Further

1. What is made clear in the following verses?
    2 Chronicles 36:14-16
    John 3:19-21, Sunday's gospel

2. What is a common error that is stated in Jeremiah 5:12-13?

3. What are the consequences of Israel's sin according to 2 Chronicles 36:17-21?

4. What is the hope given in 2 Chronicles 36:22-23?

5. What is the hope Jesus explains to Nicodemus in Sunday's gospel John 3:14-15?

Reflection

1. In our day, how does God call us back from sin, teach us truth, and show us His way?

2. Over the past decade, many scandals involving Christians have been in the media. How do these scandals affect your faith? Why is it good these sins are brought to light? How does this purifying process in God's household give hope? How can you seek the light and live in the light?

3. The prophets and messengers of God in the time of Chronicles and in Jesus' time were put to death for speaking truth and bringing light to darkness. How can your life be a source of light?

4. Can you think of a time that you turned to God and repented because of the consequences of your action? What are some things we can learn by experiencing consequences for our sin?

Optional Exercise. Have each person in the group briefly share about an event from his or her past week or about an upcoming event. This could be a time to share a triumph, trial, or need.

Second Reading

Ephesians 2:4-10

Setting the Stage

The second reading is from the letter of St. Paul to the Ephesians. This is a circular letter written in about A.D. 100 to the Christians living around Ephesus (modern-day southwestern Turkey). These are the words of God our Father telling us of His plan for our happiness. And we hear the answer to the big question about forgiveness: Do we have to earn it?

Read the second reading aloud. Reread this Scripture. What word, phrase, or idea stands out for you?

Exploring Further

1. How does God show His mercy and love?
   Ephesians 2:4-6
   John 3:16-17, Sunday's gospel

2. What do the following verses make clear regarding our condition and contribution to salvation and forgiveness?
   Ephesians 2:5, 8-9
   Colossians 2:13-14
   Titus 3:4-7

3. Salvation and forgiveness are free gifts. What does receiving this gift call us to according to Ephesians 2:10?

4. What light do the following Scriptures shed on the good works we are called to?
   Ephesians 4:11-13
   2 Corinthians 5:17-20

Reflection

The following story is paraphrased from a homily by Fr. Les Drewicki.

Once there was a man who worked for a large firm. He stole from the firm and was found out and knew he would be fired. The senior partner called him in and asked about what he had done. After the man confessed to his stealing, the senior partner said, "If I forgive you and let you keep your job, will I be able to trust you?"

The shocked employee responded, "Yes. You can trust me until the day I die." The senior partner continued, "What you did, I did. The mercy I extend to you was extended to me."

1. Can you think of a time when someone extended forgiveness to you? What effect did this have on your life? Have you ever extended forgiveness to someone else? What were the results? Can you think of someone you need to forgive? What steps can you take to put this into action?

2. How does working together bond a family or group? How does your work in church, home, or community give you a sense of belonging? How can we foster an attitude of all we do is a response to all Jesus did for us?

3. What are some "good works" that you have been given to do? Do you consider this a duty or a privilege? If you are not involved in some area of service, what holds you back?

Closing Prayer

Lord, help us to be merciful to one another, as You are merciful to us. Amen.

FIFTH SUNDAY OF LENT
YEAR B

Note For parishes engaged in the RCIA, this Sunday is the third scrutiny. The readings from the fifth Sunday of Lent year C-A, "Come and Drink," will be read.

Opening Song

Opening Prayer

Open in prayer and invite everyone to add his or her own prayer. Close together: Create in me a clean heart, O God, and put a new and right spirit in me. Amen. (Psalm 51:10)

Review Study Guidelines

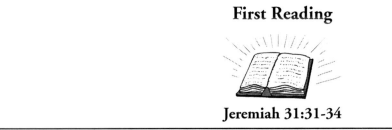

First Reading

Jeremiah 31:31-34

Setting the Stage

The first reading is from the book of the prophet Jeremiah. Jeremiah lives about 550 years before Jesus, during the time of the deportation of the Hebrew people by the Babylonians to what is now Iraq. Seven hundred years earlier, the ancestors of the Hebrews are in a dark moment, too; they are slaves in Egypt. God has established with them a special and close relationship called a "covenant," similar to a marriage. Note the names: "house of Israel"—this refers to people of the northern part of Palestine, and "house of Judah"—this refers to the people of the southern part. The old covenant is the Ten Commandments written on stone tablets; what will the new covenant, the New Testament, be written on?

Read the first reading aloud. Reread this Scripture. What word, phrase, or idea stands out for you?

Exploring Further

1. Why did the old covenant fail?
    Jeremiah 31:32
    Ezekiel 16:59-60

2. What is God's plan for a new covenant according to Jeremiah 31:33?

3. What does the new covenant say regarding forgiveness?
    Jeremiah 31:34
    Ezekiel 16:62-63

4. In the new covenant, who will be responsible for sin according to Jeremiah 31:29-30?

5. How will the new covenant be made known?
    Jeremiah 31:33
    Ezekiel 36:26-27
    2 Corinthians 3:2-3

    Note: In summary, the covenant is new in three respects:[52]
    1. God's spontaneous forgiveness of sin.
    2. Individual responsibility and retribution.
    3. Interiorization of religion: the Law is to be no longer a code regulating external activity but an inspiration working on the human heart, under the influence of the Spirit of God, who gives a new heart, capable of "knowing" God.

6. How is this new covenant inaugurated according to Matthew 26:27-28?

Reflection

1. How does having God's law written on our hearts, as opposed to written on stone tablets, make a difference to living out our faith?

2. What picture does a spontaneously forgiving God bring to your mind? For you, is it hard or easy to picture God in this way? Explain.

3. Under the influence of the Spirit of God—who gives us a new heart—we are capable of "knowing" God. How have you experienced "knowing God"? How can we grow and deepen in our relationship with God?

Optional Exercise. Have each person in the group briefly share about an event from his or her past week or about an upcoming event. This could be a time to share a triumph, trial, or need.

Second Reading

Hebrews 5:7-9

Setting the Stage

The second reading is from the letter to the Hebrews, written about A.D. 70 by a Jew who has become a Christian. He writes to other Hebrews who have also become Christians. He wants to help them persevere in their newfound faith in Jesus. Here the writer describes their new High Priest praying in the Garden of Gethsemane. What is the result of His prayer? And who has He become for us?

Read the second reading aloud. Reread this Scripture. What word, phrase, or idea stands out for you?

Exploring Further

1. What does Jesus do and why is He heard according to Hebrews 5:7?

2. When does Jesus offer up prayers with loud cries and tears in Luke 22:41-44?

3. What does Jesus learn through suffering according to Hebrews 5:8?

4. Who is looking for Jesus and what might this indicate in Sunday's gospel John 12:20-22?

    Note: These are possible converts to Judaism or God fearing Gentiles. It points to the message being proclaimed to the whole world.

5. How will the world have access to Jesus according to John 12:23-24?

6. What message is given to Greeks and those "wanting to see Jesus" in John 12:25-26?

7. When the task is hard, how does Jesus respond in John 12:27-28a, Sunday's gospel?

8. What is the result of Jesus suffering and laying down his life?
    John 12:28-33
    Hebrews 5:9

    Note: "Christ was always morally perfect. In the Bible, perfection usually means completeness or maturity. By sharing our suffering, Christ shared our human experience completely."[53]

Reflection

1. Jesus obeys even when it leads to death. How can Jesus help us even when obedience is difficult? Can you think of a time in which you suffered because of your obedience to God?

2. When Jesus was on earth, at one point the people wanted to make Him king, but Jesus refused. God had a bigger plan. To Jesus' disciples, Jesus suffering and dying seemed like defeat. God had a bigger plan—salvation of the whole world. Can you think of a time in your life when you prayed for a trial or hardship to be removed and it wasn't, or your hopes and plans were dashed but in looking back you can glimpse some of the "bigger plan" God had for you, your family, or your church? Explain. Maybe right now you are in a situation that is not going the way you would like. How might God be working out something bigger?

3. Do you think that obedience in the midst of suffering is a true test of faith? Why or why not? What does the fact that Jesus shared in our human experience, even suffering, mean to you?

4. Whose life demonstrates faithfulness in the midst of suffering? How does this affect your faith?

Closing Prayer

We are grateful Lord that You are an understanding and merciful high priest. Thank you for being the sacrifice that covered our sins. Amen.

Passion Sunday
Year B

Opening Song

Opening Prayer

Open in prayer and invite everyone to add his or her own prayer. Close together: Hosanna in the highest. Blessed are You who come to bring mercy and life. Amen.

Review Study Guidelines

First Reading

Isaiah 50:4-7

Setting the Stage

The first reading is from the book of the prophet Isaiah. These words are first spoken about 540 years before Jesus. The Jewish people have been deported to Babylon (modern-day Iraq) two years earlier. The person we hear speaking is called "servant of the Lord." This title can refer either to an individual or a teacher sent to bring encouragement, or it can be a symbol of the whole group suffering in exile. For Christians today, we can also see a description of the One who suffered for us on the cross.

Read the first reading aloud. Reread this Scripture. What word, phrase, or idea stands out for you?

Exploring Further

1. What impact can a word from a teacher have according to Isaiah 50:4a?

2. What do the following Scriptures say regarding words and their effect?
   Proverbs 12:18
   Proverbs 12:25
   Proverbs 16:24

3. What do the following Scriptures tell us about the Word of Jesus?
   John 5:24, 28-29a
   John 11:43-44
   John 12:49-50
   John 17:17

4. How does the servant in Isaiah 50:4b-5 start the day?

5. When the servant acts in obedience, what is result?
   Isaiah 50:6-7
   Mark 14:10, 17-20, 43-46, 50, Sunday's gospel
   Mark 14:55-58, Sunday's gospel
   Mark 14:66-72, Sunday's gospel
   Mark 15:6-20, Sunday's gospel
   Mark 15:25-30, Sunday's gospel

6. What gives the servant hope in dealing with abuse?
   Isaiah 50:7
   Psalm 25:2-3

7. How does Jesus help the woman and keep her from being disgraced in Sunday's gospel Mark 14:1-9?

Reflection

1. Isaiah is awakened by the Lord each morning. What awakens you in the morning? What difference does it make when you start your day by listening to God in prayer?

2. Can you think of a time someone gave you a word of encouragement when you were weary or discouraged? What difference did it make? Can you think of someone who may need a word or note of encouragement?

3. Have you ever been laughed at, reviled, or rejected? How did you respond? Have you ever laughed at, reviled, or rejected someone else—possibly of another race, culture, religion, or outside your circle of friends—through jokes or stories?

4. Can you think of anyone in your community, province, or country who is being laughed at, reviled, or rejected? What is one change in attitude or one action we can make to stand with Jesus among the dominated, excluded, marginalized, and poor?

5. On Passion Sunday we remember the suffering of Jesus. Death on a cross was considered scandalous and a mark of being cursed by God. Instead of responding in power and vindication, God seemed silent. How hard it must have been for the followers of Jesus to trust and believe God in the face of these events! Have you experienced hard situations where God seemed to be absent or silent? What did you do? What was helpful? In hindsight, can you see God in this situation?

Optional Exercise. Have each person in the group briefly share about an event from his or her past week or about an upcoming event. This could be a time to share a triumph, trial, or need.

Second Reading

Philippians 2:5-11

Setting the Stage
The second reading is from the letter of St. Paul to the church at Philippi, northern Greece. He is writing from a prison perhaps in western Turkey about 30 years after the resurrection of Jesus. The Philippian church sent help to Paul, and he writes to thank them and encourage them in their faith. This reading is actually a quote from an early Christian hymn. Through these words, whose attitude is God our Father calling us to imitate?

Read the second reading aloud. Reread this Scripture. What word, phrase, or idea stands out for you?

Exploring Further

1. How does Jesus demonstrate humility and obedience?
    Philippians 2:6-8
    Mark 15:33-37, Sunday's gospel

2. How might we imitate Jesus in letting go of our rights and serving?
    Philippians 2:3-4
    Acts 5:41
    Romans 15:1-2
    Hebrews 12:1-2

3. How is Jesus glorified following His humility and obedience in Philippians 2:9-11?

4. If we believe and profess Jesus, what reward are we promised in Romans 10:10-13

Reflection

1. If the attitude of unity, selflessness, humility, putting others first, and obedience were lived out at home, at work, and in your church, what difference would it make? What is one thing you can do to work toward this goal?

2. We remember Jesus' passion this time of year and recall the extreme humiliation Jesus accepted. What is the difference between humility and being a doormat? How can we grow in humility? Can you trust Jesus will never let you be put to shame, and what difference does this make to you?

3. Can you think of situations where individuals or groups draw a great deal of attention as they demand their rights? What are the results? Can you think of an individual or group who serves, receiving little or no recognition? What effect does their service have?

4. Can you name some people or groups who are dominated, excluded, marginalized, or forgotten? What can you do to speak for them?

Closing Prayer

Lord, You humbled yourself for our sake. May we follow Your example and share in Your resurrection. Amen.

SECTION FIVE

EASTER

Easter is the culmination of our faith, hopes, beliefs, and dreams.

We celebrate Easter for 50 days. The number "49" [7 x 7] stands for the fullness of time for the Jewish people. The church adds a day to show that Easter is greater than the fullness of time. We need the 40 days of Lent to empty ourselves and prepare in order to recognize and celebrate the 50 days of Easter.

A number of years ago, my good friend Gail said that believers are usually willing to fast and do penance for forty days, but we are not up to celebrating for fifty days. It is hard to sustain the celebration because we do not really grasp what it means to be Easter people. We are more comfortable with the cross and the pain of life than the hope and freedom of the resurrection. Gail decided that every Easter season she would pick pussy willows so she could display fresh flowers throughout her house during Easter as a reminder to continue the celebration. A few years after she began the practice, she died from cancer. But if you come to my house during the Easter season, you'll see pussy willows and fresh flowers spread throughout as a way to celebrate Gail's resurrection, and to serve as a reminder that I am part of a "resurrection people."

Easter teaches us that even in the face of pain, suffering, and death we believe in things not yet seen. We have a sure hope in the promises of life, hope, salvation, and joy.

I want to challenge you to be an Easter person, an alleluia person, to be full of hope and joy because Jesus has risen! Indeed, he has risen. So will we. Celebrate the six Sundays of Easter, Ascension Sunday, and Pentecost. Celebrate for 50 days!

After Easter we are led back into ordinary time by two more feast days. First, we have Trinity Sunday when we are reminded that our one God subsists in Three Persons, the Father, Son, and Holy Spirit. The Trinity gives us the perfect example of living in a loving community which always produces life. The second feast day is that of the Body and Blood of Christ, or Corpus Christi Sunday. At this feast we remember how we are nourished and sustained for the spiritual journey.

This brings us full circle—back to ordinary time; the daily routine that is so necessary to the faith journey. Here we develop life lessons of prayer, study, and service, gathering as a people. In routine, we develop a foundational relationship with God, strengthening us to stand firm during times of celebration and sorrow.

By His great mercy
He has given us a new birth
into a living hope
through the resurrection of Jesus
from the dead.

(1 Peter 1:3)

Easter Sunday
Year B

Opening Song

Opening Prayer

Open in prayer and invite everyone to add his or her own prayer. Close together: Father, by sending Your Son to suffer and die and then by raising Him to life, You opened the way of eternal life for us. Amen.

Note: To celebrate Easter, we have a rich banquet of Scripture readings—eight readings from the Vigil and another three to choose from on Easter Sunday, not counting the Psalms and Gospels! Every parish chooses from these readings. As it is impossible to study all the readings in one lesson, we will study only the first reading of the Easter Sunday Mass. This reading summarizes the gospel in a wonderfully concise way, thus we can focus on why we celebrate this most holy feast.

Review Study Guidelines

First Reading

Acts 10:34, 36-43

Setting the Stage

This first reading is from the Acts of the Apostles. We hear of an event in the life of St. Peter that takes place about ten years[54] after the resurrection of Jesus. St. Peter is called to the home of a Roman military officer called Cornelius. He is a prayerful man who has asked relatives and close friends to gather to hear St. Peter. We listen now to what is said to them. They become the first converts who are not Jews. As you read this, consider what happens to people who come to believe in the Risen Jesus.

Note: Perhaps the greatest barrier to the spread of the gospel in the first century was the Jewish-Gentile conflict. Most early believers were Jewish, and to them it was scandalous even to think of associating with Gentiles. But God told Peter to take the gospel to a Roman, and Peter obeyed despite his background and personal feelings.'[55]

Read the first reading aloud. Reread this Scripture. What word, phrase, or idea stands out for you?

Exploring Further

1. What does Peter realize according to Acts 10:34-35?

2. What is the message brought to the people of Israel according to Acts 10:36?

3. What is said concerning those who bring good news in Isaiah 52:7?

4. What events does Peter recall in Acts 10:37-38?

5. What do the following Scriptures say about Jesus' anointing, power, and mission?
    Matthew 3:16-17
    Matthew 8: 28-32

    By his power over demons, Jesus destroys the empire of Satan and inaugurates the messianic kingdom characterized by the Holy Spirit. Even if Israel refuses to recognize Jesus, demons have no doubt about him. This power of exorcism is communicated by Jesus to his disciples at the same time as the power of miraculous cures.[56]

    Luke 4:18-20
    Acts 2:22

6. What is part of the function of an apostle?
    Acts 10:39a
    Acts 1:21-22

7. What were the apostles a witness, too?
    Acts: 10:39b-41
    John 19:28-30, 33-35
    Luke 24:36-43
    Acts 1:3-4

8. What does Mary Magdalene witness in Sunday's gospel, John 20:1-2, 10-18?

9. What are the disciples commanded to do?
    Acts 10:42
    Matthew 28:18-20

10. What is the promise attached in Matthew 28:20?

11. What is the good news for everyone?
    Acts 10:43
    Acts 2:38-39

Reflection

1. Peter has to put aside beliefs and prejudices he was raised with in order to go to Cornelius' home. How can we recognize and put aside our prejudices toward other languages, culture, different economic classes, education, etc., to share the good news of Jesus with love?

2. Can you think of barriers that make it hard for you to believe God can break through and bring truth, love, freedom, etc., to you, another person, or a specific situation? Explain.

3. Who has been a "beautiful messenger" to you, bringing peace, hope, encouragement, and support?

4. Everything God the Father gave to Jesus, Jesus gave to us. We have been given a share in His blessings and His mission (see Luke 4:18-19 and 28:18-20). How are you or how can you live out His mission in your life?

5. Often we hear of Jesus' life, death, and resurrection. This truth can become so familiar that we forget the startling reality of what it means. As a group, list the changes and blessings in your lives that you have experienced by believing in Jesus.

Closing Prayer

Spend some time thanking God for what His Son means to you.

SECOND SUNDAY OF EASTER
YEAR B
DIVINE MERCY SUNDAY

Opening Song

Opening Prayer

Open in prayer and invite everyone to add his or her own prayer. Close together: Father, for the sake of Your Son's sorrowful passion and death, have mercy on us. Amen.

Review Study Guidelines

First Reading

Acts 4:32-35

Setting the Stage

The first reading is from the Acts of the Apostles written by St. Luke about 40 years after the resurrection of Jesus. We hear a quick summary, not a historically exact picture, of the first Christian church in Jerusalem. It answers the very important question: Does belief in Jesus affect the way we look on others, especially those in need?

Read the first reading aloud. Reread this Scripture. What word, phrase, or idea stands out for you?

Exploring Further

1. How are the early Christians described in Acts 4:32?

2. What further picture do we have of the early church and what may have contributed to its unity in Acts 2:42-47?

3. What is Jesus' prayer for his followers in John 17:20-23?

4. How important is unity to the early church as expressed by Paul in Philippians 2:1-2?

5. What do the apostles continue to testify to in Acts 4:33?

6. What did they experience that became part of their testimony, as described in Sunday's gospel, John 20:19-23?

7. What accompanies the apostles' testimony and validates it according to Acts 5:12-16

8. People believe the apostles' testimony. What does Jesus say about believing what you have heard without seeing in Sunday's gospel, John 20:26-29?

9. In what practical ways did they care for each other in Acts 4:34-35?

10. What do we learn regarding this kind of generosity with possessions in Luke 12:33-34?

Reflection

1. Believers are called to be of one heart and mind, sharing everything. Where have you experienced the greatest unity and sharing of self and possessions?

2. How important do you think Christian unity is to God? What contributes to disunity among Christians? How can you make a difference for unity?

3. Do signs and wonders still happen in the name of Jesus? Explain. Are signs and wonders important? Why or why not? What signs and wonders have you experienced?

4. How attached to your possessions are you? In what way are you willing to share with those in need? What could several families co-own and share? What would the advantages and disadvantages be?

5. As Canadians, what is our obligation to share with refugees? How can we assist those in want within our country? In other countries?

Optional Exercise. Have each person in the group briefly share about an event from his or her past week or about an upcoming event. This could be a time to share a triumph, trial, or need.

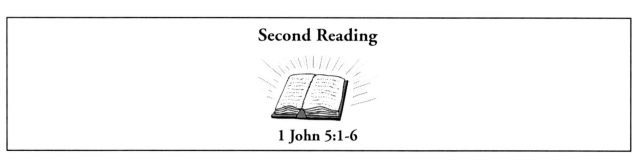

Second Reading

1 John 5:1-6

Setting the Stage

This reading is from the first letter of John. This is written around A.D. 100 to the different Christian churches in the Roman province called Asia (modern-day western Turkey).[57] Tradition says that this is where St. John the Apostle worked. These churches are facing the problem of heresy. Some Christians are saying that Jesus was born a human and baptized, but He did not die on the cross. They cannot accept that a Divine Person could die. Note: God our Father is telling us the many different ways we can express our faith.

Read the second reading aloud. Reread this Scripture. What word, phrase, or idea stands out for you?

Exploring Further

1. How do we become a child of God according to 1 John 5:1a?

2. What do following Scriptures teach about love?
    1 John 5:1b
    Romans 13:8-10

3. What shows our love according to 1 John 5:3?

4. How are God's requirements beautifully summed up in Micah 6:8?

5. God's commandments are not meant to be burdensome but to do what?
    1 John 5:3b-4
    John 15:10-11
    Matthew 11:29-30

6. What overcomes the "world" according to 1 John 5:5?

    NOTE: The word "world" is used in three ways in Scripture:
    1. *World* can refer to the physical creation and it is used this way in Genesis.[58]
    2. *World* can refer to all who are hostile to God; all that stands in enmity with God. Love of the world reflects attachment to what is transitory. Love of God brings Christians into relationship with what "remains" forever. Examples are found in 1 John.[59]
    3. *World* can refer to people in general. It is used this way in John 3:16; "For God so loved the *world* that he sent his only Son, so that everyone who believes in him may not perish but may have eternal life."

7. What meaning of "world" is used in this reading?

8. To defend against the heresy that said Jesus is not a Divine Person at his death on the cross, what does John say were the three witnesses to Jesus in 1 John 5:6-8?

    Note that water refers to the baptism of Jesus, blood refers to His blood shed on the cross, and spirit refers to the Holy Spirit.

Reflection

1. When we believe in Jesus Christ, we become a child of God. In what ways can we treat all believers as genuine brothers and sisters in the family of God? Explain.

2. What convinced you to accept Jesus, the Son of God, as your Lord and Saviour? How has your understanding of God's love as "divine mercy" grown or changed?

3. Who was a witness for you in accepting faith in Jesus Christ?

4. How has your faith made a difference in overcoming worldly attachments, wrong relationships, wrong attitudes, or other struggles?

Closing Prayer

Father, through our belief in the resurrection of Your Son, we become Your children. May we know the abundant love and mercy You pour out on us Your children and draw ever closer to this great love and mercy. Alleluia.

Third Sunday of Easter
Year B

Opening Song

Opening Prayer

Open in prayer and invite everyone to add his or her own prayer. Close together: God our Father, Your light of truth guides us to the way of Christ. Amen.

Review Study Guidelines

First Reading

Acts 3:13-15, 17-19

Setting the Stage

The first reading is from the Acts of the Apostles written by St. Luke about 40 years after the resurrection of Jesus. We hear St. Peter speaking to the people who gather after his first miracle. In the name of Jesus, he has cured a crippled man at the entrance to the temple in Jerusalem. The good news for us is the answer to the question: Is God our Father willing to forgive sin?

Read the first reading aloud. Reread this Scripture. What word, phrase, or idea stands out for you?

Exploring Further

1. What miracle occurs in Acts 3:1-2, 5-8?

2. What follows the miracle in Acts 3:11?

3. How does God say to address the people in His name in Exodus 3:15?

4. What does Peter remind the people of in Acts 3:14?

5. What crimes are Jesus and Barabbas accused of and what is the result?
   Luke 23:2, 5
   Luke 23:18-20, 22-25

6. How does God have the final say in Acts 3:15-16?

7. Why do the people kill the "author of life"?
   Acts 3:17
   1 Corinthians 2:8

8. What was foretold through the prophets?
   Acts 3:18
   Luke 18:31-32

9. Even though it was foretold through the prophets and Jesus told the disciples what would happen, how do they respond when they encounter the resurrected Jesus in Sunday's gospel Luke 24:35-40?

10. Once we know the truth, how are we exhorted to respond in Acts 3:19-20?

11. What helps the disciples to understand in Luke 24:41-45?

12. What are the disciple called to according to Luke 24:46-49?

Reflection

1. The healing of the crippled man caught the attention of the people and they gathered to hear more. What caught your attention and stirred your interest to know more about your faith?

2. Peter took advantage of the situation and proclaimed the gospel message. When have you recognized an opportunity to share faith? What are possible opportunities in everyday life for you to share your faith?

3. Today's Scriptures point out that ignorance and unbelief are the reasons we rejected and persecuted the author of life. How have you acted in ignorance and unbelief toward your faith or aspects of it? How has experiencing a relationship with Jesus changed your thinking? How have you made changes in your life as a result of a growing faith?

4. Jesus appeared to the disciples and opened their minds to understand His teaching. Today, how does Jesus continue to reveal Himself and open our minds to truth? What does an encounter with the resurrected Jesus call us to do?

Optional Exercise. Have each person in the group briefly share about an event from his or her past week or about an upcoming event. This could be a time to share a triumph, trial, or need.

Second Reading

1 John 2:1-5

Setting the Stage

The next reading is from the first letter of John, written about 70 years after the resurrection of Jesus to the Christians in western Turkey, where St. John the Apostle is said to have worked. God our Father is answering this question: When we sin, to whom should we turn?

Read the second reading aloud. Reread this Scripture. What word, phrase, or idea stands out for you?

Exploring Further

1. Who is John writing to and why according to 1 John 2:1?

2. What has Jesus done and for whom according to 1 John 2:2?

3. How can we be sure that we know Jesus according to 1 John 2:3-4?

4. What is the result of obedience and what is the proof of obedience in 1 John 2:5-6?

Reflection

1. When you sin, is your first response to confess it or to justify your sin? Jesus has atoned for our sins and when we confess we are *forgiven* and *cleansed*. What does this mean to you personally and how do you make use of this gift?

2. Is there someone in your life you need to forgive or ask forgiveness from? What steps can you take to begin this reconciliation process?

3. This knowledge is faith and embraces a whole way of life in such a way that conduct is the criterion by which life in Christ may be recognized.[60] If you were on trial for being a Christian by your conduct, what evidence would there be to convict you?

4. As a church, where do we need to ask forgiveness for lacking in love, fellowship, or poor conduct? As a church we are corporately the body of Christ. What is our responsibility in reflecting the love of God by how we act, love, and serve?

Closing Prayer

Father, may they know we belong to You by witnessing the love we have for one another. Amen

Fourth Sunday of Easter
Year B

Opening Song

Opening Prayer

Open in prayer and invite everyone to add his or her own prayer. Close together: Give thanks to the Lord for he is good; His steadfast love endures forever. Amen. (Psalm 118)

Review Study Guidelines

First Reading

Acts 4:1-3, 7-12

Setting the Stage

The first reading is from the Acts of the Apostles written by St. Luke about 40 years after the resurrection of Jesus. The first miracle that St. Peter works is the healing of a crippled man. Last Sunday we heard him explain that miracle to the people; today we hear him talk about it to the religious authorities. He uses the phrase "the stone that was rejected." This is a quote from Psalm 118. God our Father tells us who we should turn to when we are rejected or crippled in body or in heart.

Read the first reading aloud. Reread this Scripture. What word, phrase, or idea stands out for you?

Exploring Further

1. What three groups come upon John and Peter as they are speaking to the people in Acts 4:1?

    Note: The priests were the chief priests who had special influence and were often close relatives of the high priests. The captain of the temple was the leader of the temple police, who were guards set around the temple to ensure order. The Sadducees were members of small but powerful Jewish religious sect who did not believe in the resurrection of the dead...Even under Roman rule, the Sadducees had almost unlimited power over the temple grounds. Thus they were able to arrest Peter and John for no reason other than teaching something that contradicted their beliefs.[61]

2. What are Peter and John teaching and what is the result in Acts 4:2-3?

3. According to Peter, how was the crippled person healed in Acts 4:8-10?

4. How does this fulfill Jesus' words in Acts 1:8?

5. According to the following Scriptures, what happens when the name of Jesus is invoked?
   John 14:13-14
   Acts 2:21
   Acts 3:6
   Acts 16:16-18

   Note: The "name," according to the ancients, is inseparable from the person and shares his prerogatives.[62]

6. What is the result of calling on the name of Jesus according to Acts 4:12?

7. Why can we trust Jesus according to Sunday's gospel John 10:14-15, 17-18?

8. The rulers, elders, and scribes assembled are familiar with the Psalms. What is foretold in Psalm 118:21-23?

9. How does Paul say this is fulfilled in Acts 4:11?

10. What results when we come to the cornerstone according to 1 Peter 2:4-7a?

11. What results and why according to 1 Peter 2:7b-8?

Reflection

1. The disciples are arrested for proclaiming Jesus. Today, where are people imprisoned for practicing their faith? Would you go to Sunday worship each week if there were the possibility that you and/or the pastor could be arrested? Explain.

2. To those who trust and believe, Jesus is precious. To those who disobey, Jesus is a stumbling block. In our day, how is Jesus Christ a stumbling block?

3. Peter is filled with the Holy Spirit and speaks out in boldness. How have you experienced acting in boldness, praying with someone, speaking to someone, or sharing your faith? Explain.

4. The cornerstone (or crowning stone) has now been in place for over 2,000 years. What is an example during these 2,000 years in which we, as the church, have "let ourselves be living stones built by him"? What might be examples of not allowing ourselves to be used as living stones for God?

5. What acts have you witnessed or experienced "in the name of Jesus"?

Optional Exercise. Have each person in the group briefly share about an event from his or her past week or about an upcoming event. This could be a time to share a triumph, trial, or need.

Second Reading

1 John 3:1-3

Setting the Stage
The next reading is from the first letter of John written around A.D. 100 to Christians in what is now western Turkey, where tradition says St. John the Apostle worked. Through these words, God our Father answers these questions: 1. Who are we as human beings? 2. What is our future?

Read the second reading aloud. Reread this Scripture. What word, phrase, or idea stands out for you?

Exploring Further

1. What great love is lavished on us according to 1 John 3:1?

2. How do we become children of God according to John 1:12?

3. How does Jesus show us His love and care for us according to Sunday's gospel, John 10:11-13?

4. What is the relationship of God's children with Jesus, as revealed in John 10:14-15?

5. What does Jesus reveal in John 10:16?

6. What do the children of God receive according to Romans 8:14-17?

7. We are children of God now. What will we become according to 1 John 3:2a?

8. What hints do the following Scriptures give about what is to come?
    1 John 3:2b
    Matthew 22:30
    1 Corinthians 15:49-53
    Philippians 3:20-21
    Colossians 3:2-4

Reflection

1. What does being a child of God mean to you? How have you experienced the Father's love?

2. What is your understanding of "what we will become"?

3. Whenever Scripture says "know" God, it means *experience* God. What is your experience of the Good Shepherd?

Closing Prayer

Thank you Father for loving us and making us Your children. Good Shepherd, thank You for laying down Your life for us. Amen.

Fifth Sunday of Easter
Year B

Opening Song

Opening Prayer

Open in prayer and invite everyone to add his or her own prayer. Close together: Lord, help us to speak out boldly, proclaiming Your name and praising You to all people. Amen.

Review Study Guidelines

First Reading

Acts 9:26-31

Setting the Stage
The first reading is from the Acts of the Apostles written by St. Luke about 40 years after the resurrection of Jesus. Today we hear what happens to St. Paul after his conversion. Not only does his life change, but his name changes from "Saul" to "Paul." It is interesting to know he is born in a city called Tarsus, in what is now southeastern Turkey, and is only about 25 years old when he is touched by Jesus—about six years after His resurrection.

> Note: "Hellenists" are Jews who could only speak Greek. The expression "fear of the Lord" means "respect," "awe," and "reverence."

In this story of St. Paul, God our Father answers the question: Is the impossible possible?

Read the first reading aloud. Reread this Scripture. What word, phrase, or idea stands out for you?

Exploring Further

1. When Paul attempts to join the disciples in Jerusalem, what happens in Acts 9:26?

2. What reason do the Christians have to fear Paul?
   Acts 8:1
   Acts 9:1-2

3. Who speaks up for Paul and how in Acts 9:27?

4. What results after Barnabas gives Paul a characteristic reference in Acts 9:28?

5. How is Paul received by some Jews and how does the Jerusalem church deal with this in Acts 9:29?

6. What is the state of the church at this time according to Acts 9:31?

Reflection

1. Barnabas speaks favourably of Paul, opening the way for his acceptance in Jerusalem and giving Paul a chance for others to see how he has changed. How have you been helped by someone believing in you, speaking for you, or including you? Do you know anyone who needs a second chance? How can we be like Barnabas for others?

2. Paul was transformed by his encounter with the living Jesus. How has your encounter with Jesus transformed you? How has your conversion been received by others?

Optional Exercise. Have each person in the group briefly share about an event from his or her past week or about an upcoming event. This could be a time to share a triumph, trial, or need.

Second Reading

1 John 3:18-24

Setting the Stage
The next reading is from the first letter of John written around A.D. 100 to Christians in what is now western Turkey, where St. John the Apostle is said to have worked. Through these words, God our Father tells us what it means to be a Christian.

Read the second reading aloud. Reread this Scripture. What word, phrase, or idea stands out for you?

Exploring Further

1. What is the standard of love Jesus set and asks of us in 1 John 3:16?

2. What should love do according to 1 John 3:17-18?

3. What is the result of love in action according to 1 John 3:19-20?

4. How is the difference between talk and action further emphasized in Matthew 7:21?

5. What enables us to obey and live in love according to Sunday's gospel John 15:1-6?

6. What is the condition to receiving what we ask for according to 1 John 3:21-22?

7. What is the twofold commandment given in 1 John 3:23?

8. What is the result of keeping this commandment?
   1 John 3:24a
   John 15:7-8, Sunday's gospel

9. What is the proof of this unity with God in 1 John 3:24b?

10. What result of receiving the Spirit is made clear in Galatians 4:6-7?

Reflection

1. Sharing our material possessions with those in need illustrates love in action, according to 1 John 3. Where do you see a need that you can contribute to?

2. We are clearly commanded to believe in Jesus and love one another. This results in unity with God and with one another. Can you think of a situation(s) in which unity is less than God would desire? What one thing can you do to work toward unity in this situation?

3. How can we "lay down our lives" for others in everyday life? How can you show love to someone you will encounter this week?

4. How can we abide in the true vine, Jesus? How does Jesus prune us so we can bear more fruit?

Closing Prayer

Lord, continue to work in our lives so that we will be known as Your children. Amen.

SIXTH SUNDAY OF EASTER
YEAR B

Opening Song

Opening Prayer

Open in prayer and invite everyone to add his or her own prayer. Close together: God, we believe in the resurrection of our Lord. Help us to express in our lives and to celebrate what we believe. Amen.

Review Study Guidelines

First Reading

Acts 10:25-26, 34-35, 44-48

Setting the Stage

The first reading is from the Acts of the Apostles written by St. Luke about A.D. 70. Today's reading describes an important episode in the life of St. Peter. Notice that it happens more than ten years after the resurrection of Jesus. St. Peter, being a Jewish Christian, still follows strict Jewish laws—such as not visiting or eating with persons who are not Jews. Then God our Father tells him in a vision that those laws have to change. God then sends Peter to visit a man called Cornelius, who is not a Jew; in fact, he is an officer in the Roman occupation army stationed in Caesarea, near Tel Aviv today. So, to whom does He send His Holy Spirit?

Read the first reading aloud. Reread this Scripture. What word, phrase, or idea stands out for you?

Exploring Further

1. How does Cornelius, a Roman army officer, greet Peter's arrival in Acts 10:25?

2. What is Peter's response in Acts 10:26?

3. Why do people want to worship the messenger and what is the consistent response to this?
   Acts 14:8-15
   Revelation 19:9-10

4. What does Peter understand about God in Acts 10:34?

5. On what terms does God accept people according to Acts 10:35?

6. What happens to the Gentiles while Peter is still speaking in Acts 10:44-45, and what is the reaction of the Jewish believers?

7. How do they know the Spirit fell on the Gentiles in Acts 10:46?

8. In the following Scriptures, what difference does receiving the Holy Spirit make?
   Acts 1:8, John 15:26-27, 2 Timothy 1:6-8
   Acts 2:4, Acts 11:27-28, 1 Corinthians 12:4-11
   Acts 8:29-31, 36-40, and Acts 10:19-29

9. After the Gentiles receive the Holy Spirit, what does Peter decide in Acts 10:47-48?

10. What do the new Gentile believers ask of Peter in Acts 10:48b?

11. How is Peter's stay with the new believers greeted by the Hebrew believers in Judea according to Acts 11:1-3?

Reflection

1. Consider your position at home, church, work, and in groups you belong to. What possibilities exist to misuse your position for possible power, pride, or prestige? Think of leaders and talented people you admire. What are ways we can put them on "pedestals"? How can we support them?

2. What would be characteristics of a church or group that "showed no partiality"? Would all people be made welcome in your Bible study and in your church? Explain.

3. The Jerusalem community are more shocked that Peter lodged with the uncircumcised Gentiles than they are that he baptized them. How can prejudice, fear, a narrow understanding of God, or ways of thinking prevent us from seeing God at work? How can we prepare so the eyes of our heart recognize God working in unexpected ways?

Optional Exercise. Have each person in the group briefly share about an event from his or her past week or about an upcoming event. This could be a time to share a triumph, trial, or need.

Second Reading

1 John 4:7-10

Setting the Stage

The next reading is from the first letter of John written around A.D. 100 to Christians living in what is now western Turkey, where tradition says St. John the Apostle worked. God our Father is telling us where love comes from.

Read the second reading aloud. Reread this Scripture. What word, phrase, or idea stands out for you?

Exploring Further

1. What is the result of having love or not having love according to 1 John 4:7-8?

2. How is God's love made visible?
   1 John 4:9
   Romans 5:8

3. What does God's love call us to?
   1 John 4:19
   Matthew 18:23-35
   John 15:9-10, 12, Sunday's gospel

4. What results when we abide in the Father's love and keep His commandments in John 15:11?

5. What is the greatest show of love according to Sunday's gospel, John 15:13?

6. What do these Scriptures say regarding the relationship and origin of our love?
   1 John 4:10
   John 15:14-17

Reflection

1. What are some examples of sacrificial love and examples of self-centered love? Who have you known or read about that demonstrated sacrificial love?

2. Often people use the phrase "they fell in love" or "they fell out of love," or "are no longer in love." Do you think love is a feeling or a choice? Explain. When we do not feel loving toward our spouse, child, parent, church community, etc., what should we do to live out love?

3. How do you think Jesus felt when the people rejected Him, laughed at Him, whipped Him, and crucified Him? How does Jesus continue to act out His love for us despite how He must have felt?

4. In those times when we feel distanced from God, unloved, lonely, etc., how can Scripture help us to stand on truth and not on feelings?

Closing Prayer

Father, we thank You that You first loved us, making it possible to love You and one another. Amen.

Ascension Sunday
Year B

Opening Song

Opening Prayer

Open in prayer and invite everyone to add his or her own prayer. Close together: Lord, may we wait in hope for all the Father has for us. Amen.

Review Study Guidelines

First Reading

Acts 1:1-11

Setting the Stage

The first reading is from the beginning of the Acts of the Apostles, and it gives us a picture of the ascension of Jesus. We are given two biblical symbols from the Old Testament: "clouds" and "being lifted up." They are used to describe the presence of God and heaven. There is also a reference to the prophet Elisha who lives about 850 years before Jesus. Elisha is able to catch a glimpse of his teacher, the great prophet Elijah, being lifted up to heaven and so is able to have a share of his teaching spirit. Note the name "Theophilus." It is a Greek name, meaning "a lover of God." It is possibly the name of the Christian who helped St. Luke to distribute the books he wrote. In a sense, all who believe could be called "Theophilus."

Read the first reading aloud. Reread this Scripture. What word, phrase, or idea stands out for you?

Exploring Further

1. Replace "Theophilus" with "Dear friend who loves God" in Acts 1:1. Do you consider yourself included with those to whom this letter is written?

2. Luke, the author of Acts, is writing an account from the "beginning." What is the "beginning" he is referring to?
   Acts 1:1-2
   Acts 1:22

3. What are the instructions given to the apostles?
   Matthew 28:19-20
   Mark 16:15-16, Sunday's gospel

4. What signs will accompany preaching the good news according to Mark 16:17-18?

5. What does Jesus do after the resurrection according to Acts 1:3?

6. What specific orders does Jesus give in Acts 1:4-5?

7. How are we to wait for the Lord according to Psalm 130:5-6?

8. After Jesus speaks to them about the kingdom of God, what type of kingdom are the disciples still expecting in Acts 1:6?

9. The disciples still do not understand. What hope does Jesus give to them?
   Acts 1:7-8
   John 14:26

10. What happens after Jesus gives his instructions?
    Acts 1:9
    Mark 16:19-20, Sunday's gospel

11. What are the disciples doing when the two white-robed men appeared in Acts 1:10?

12. What promise does the angel give the disciples in Acts 1:11?

Reflection

1. Why is it hard to wait for God's promises? What attitudes and choices can we practice during times of waiting?

2. After the disciples received the Holy Spirit, it was time to stop "gazing into heaven" and instead implement Jesus' instructions. How might we recognize times when we are to wait on the Lord and times when we are to go forth?

3. How are you participating in this job description of a Christian to go, proclaim, baptize, teach, and remember?

4. Jesus spent time teaching the disciples about the kingdom of God and the Holy Spirit, yet the disciples were ordinary people and did not understand. Still, these are the people used to begin the church after

the ascension of Jesus. How might God use you and your church community despite your limitations? Can you think of a time in which God used you as His vessel?

5. This weekend we celebrate the ascension of Jesus into heaven and the promise of His return. Do you expect Jesus to return and are you ready?

6. The following is from a sermon by St. Augustine.[63]

> Today our Lord Jesus Christ ascended into heaven; let our hearts ascend with him. For just as he remained with us even after his ascension, so we too are already in heaven with him, even though what is promised us has not yet been fulfilled in our bodies.
>
> Why do we on earth not strive to find rest with him in heaven even now, through the faith, hope, and love that unite us to him? While in heaven he is also with us; and while on earth we are with him. He did not leave heaven when he came down to us; nor did he withdraw from us when he went up again into heaven. Christ is our head, and we are his body. No one ascended into heaven except Christ: He is the Son of Man by his union with us, and we, by our union with him are sons of God. So the Apostle says, "Just as the body is one and has many members, and all the members of the body, though many, are one body, so it is with Christ" (1 Cor. 12:12). He too has many members, but one body. Out of compassion for us he descended from heaven, and although he ascended alone, we also ascend because we are in him by grace. Thus, no one but Christ descended and no on but Christ ascended; not because these is no distinction between the head and the body, but because the body as a unity cannot be separated from the head.

•   What insights does this reflection give you on Jesus ascension and return? Explain.

Optional Exercise. Have each person in the group briefly share about an event from his or her past week or about an upcoming event. This could be a time to share a triumph, trial, or need.

Second Reading

Ephesians 4:1-13

Setting the Stage

The next reading is from the letter of St. Paul to the Ephesians. This is a letter to the Christians living around Ephesus (modern-day southwestern Turkey). Scholars are uncertain about the actual author; it is either Paul or one of his followers who, under the inspiration of the Holy Spirit, takes Paul's experiences and ideas and records them under Paul's name, toward the end of the A.D. first century. In any case, these are the words of God our Father and are special for this day because of their mention of the ascension of Jesus and the appropriate quote from Psalm 68. We hear of the work of Jesus and the Holy Spirit making us one big family, one body. How then does He want us to treat each other?

Read the second reading. Reread this Scripture. What word, phrase, or idea stands out for you?

Exploring Further

1. Paul lists three different threats to church unity.[64] The first is arguments among Christians. How can this threat be averted?
   Ephesians 4:1-3
   Colossians 3:12-15

2. The second threat is over diversity of service in the church. What needs to be understood for this threat to be averted?
   Ephesians 4:4-8, 11
   Ephesians 2:21-22
   Romans 12:4-8
   1 Corinthians 10:17

3. The third threat mentioned is unorthodox teaching. How can this threat be averted according to Ephesians 4:12-13?

4. As Christ holds the body together, how does it build itself up in love in Ephesians 4:16?

Reflection

The following excerpt is by Bishop Henry of the Calgary Diocese.[65]

… a fundamental principle of our faith, which is when we argue and reason, we honour our Creator and Redeemer who gave us minds with which to think and to draw near to Him, he said. We can never do theology well unless we have the humility and courage to listen to arguments of those with whom we disagree and take them seriously. People ponder the Word of God seeking to know God's will, not to discover evidence that God is on our side, he said. …Too often, Catholics are afraid to debate, he said. But there is no need for fear. Ever since the days of Pentecost, the Church has known tensions. The Jerusalem community–apparently of one in mind and heart–quarreled over the distribution of money and interpretation of obedience to the Law, Henry noted. …Debates and arguments are the sign of a Church which is always being renewed by the Spirit. Perfect unanimity would be a sign of the immobility of death. The purpose of pondering and studying is not simply to acquire information; it's to bring Christ to birth in the world. In talking about the Great Jubilee, Pope John Paul II has repeatedly pointed out the need for offering new opportunities for discussion and dialogue with the contemporary culture, accompanied by concrete expressions of welcome and friendship.

1. Consider the reading in Ephesians and Bishop Henry's comments. What makes it possible to have debate, dialogue, and differing opinions and still reflect love and unity as a people of God? How can differing gifts and viewpoints help the church as it does God's work?

2. What gifts do you see in those members of your study group that strengthen the whole body?

3. Can you think of a task or situation that was overwhelming for you on your own, yet with a group amazed you with what was accomplished? The mission of the church is vast. Where is working together making a difference?

Closing Prayer

Lord, through the power of Your Spirit, make us worthy of the calling to which we have been called. Amen.

Seventh Sunday of Easter (USA)
Year B

Opening Song

Opening Prayer

Open in prayer and invite everyone to add his or her own prayer. Close together: Father, grant us the grace to keep our eyes fixed on You and to trust You in all circumstances of our lives. Amen

Review Study Guidelines

First Reading

Acts 1:15-17, 20-26

Setting the Stage

The first reading is from the Acts of the Apostles written by St. Luke around the year A.D. 70. In this first chapter we hear what the first followers of Jesus did immediately after His resurrection and ascension. We hear that they find a replacement for Judas Iscariot. And through these words, God our Father gives us an idea of what to do when we need to make an important decision.

Read the first reading aloud. Reread this Scripture. What word, phrase, or idea stands out for you?

Exploring Further

1. What issue needs to be resolved in Acts 1:15-20?

2. How does Judas betray Jesus in Luke 22:47-48?

3. What does Jesus say about Judas?
   Luke 22:20-22
   John 17:12, Sunday's gospel

4. What qualifications are necessary for Judas' replacement as an apostle in Acts 1:21-22?

5. What is the role of an apostle?
   Acts 4:33
   Luke 1:1-2
   John 15:27

6. What does Jesus desire in John 17:13?

7. What does Jesus give His followers according to John 17:14?

8. What is Jesus' prayer for those He sends out to witness in Sunday's gospel, John 17:15-19?

9. Who is nominated to replace Judas as one of the twelve apostles in Acts 1:23?

10. How does God's discerning differ from humans?
    Acts 1:24-25
    Luke 16:15

11. Who is chosen as an apostle and how is the choice made in Acts 1:26?

Reflection

1. After the ascension of Jesus, the community in Jerusalem has an unresolved issue—the betrayal and death of Judas and who to choose as his replacement. Peter is direct regarding the issue and what needs to be done. This must have been a painful and emotional issue for the young community. How does your family handle difficult issues that arise? How does your church handle difficult issues that arise?

2. It is important that the apostle chosen was a witness to Jesus' baptism, life, passion, death, and resurrection. The apostle's witness is the foundation of the church. As believers we, too, are called to bear witness and be a living testimony to the risen Jesus. How can your life be a witness and testimony to Jesus?

3. The Jerusalem community acknowledged that God reads hearts and they do not. They nominated two ordinary people who met the requirements, prayed for God to choose, and then drew lots. How are people picked for positions in your church community? What points of wisdom can we draw from this reading in regards to delegating service?

4. In today's gospel, Jesus prays for His church to be protected, to have joy, to be guarded from evil, to be consecrated in truth, and to go forth to consecrate the world in truth. Jesus still prays this for the church today. If time allows, pray in this way for your families.

Optional Exercise. Have each person in the group briefly share about an event from his or her past week or about an upcoming event. This could be a time to share a triumph, trial, or need.

Second Reading

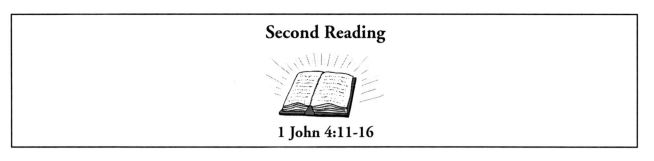

1 John 4:11-16

Setting the Stage

The next reading is from the first letter of St. John the Apostle written about 70 years after the resurrection of Jesus to Christians living in what is now western Turkey. Through these words, God our Father tells us what He is like and what He has done for us…and what kind of people He wants us to be.

Read this reading aloud. Reread this Scripture. What word, phrase, or idea stands out for you?

Exploring Further

1. What does God's love call us to?
   1 John 4:11
   Matthew 18:32-33

2. What makes God's love evident according to 1 John 4:12?

3. What do the following Scriptures say regarding "seeing" God?
   Exodus 33:20
   John 6:46

4. When will we see God?
   1 Corinthians 13:12
   1 John 3:2

5. What gives us unity with God according to 1 John 4:13?

6. What testimony is given about Jesus?
   1 John 4:14
   John 1:29
   John 4:42

7. What results when we confess that Jesus is the Son of God?
   1 John 4:15-16
   Romans 10:8-10

Reflection

1. Jesus makes God's love visible. How is our love to be made visible? What are some examples of love made visible that you have seen or heard of? How can we participate and abide in God's love?

2. What message does disunity, separation, and fighting among believers give? How do we bring love into broken relationships?

3. How have you come to believe Jesus is the Saviour of the world?

Closing Prayer

Lord, may You be glorified by our love for one another. Teach us to love as You love. Amen.

Pentecost Sunday
Year B

Opening Song

Opening Prayer

Open in prayer and invite everyone to add his or her own prayer. Close together: Come, Holy Spirit, fill us with the fire of Your love. Amen.

Review Study Guidelines

First Reading

Acts 2:1-11

Setting the Stage

The reading is from the Acts of the Apostles written by St. Luke, who wants to show the meaning of Pentecost. Jews have been celebrating Pentecost for a long time already: it is the celebration of giving their Law to Moses on Mount Sinai in the midst of fire and wind. It is there that the people are brought together as one. St. Luke wants to show that after the resurrection of Jesus, something similar but more personal and spiritual is experienced by the first Christians. We shall hear the ancient names of present-day countries beginning in the east with Iran, coming westward through Turkey and into North Africa, and finally to the capital city of the Roman Empire. The name "Asia" here refers to a Roman province in present-day Turkey. One question being address is—what effect does the Spirit have on people who are different?

Read the first reading aloud. Reread this Scripture. What word, phrase, or idea stands out for you?

Exploring Further

1. In Acts 2:1, who are referred to as "they" according to Acts 1:13-14?

2. What experience is described in Acts 2:2-3?

3. How does this fulfill John the Baptist's prophecy in Matthew 3:11?

4. What image does fire portray in the following Scriptures?
   Isaiah 5:24-25, 6:6-7, 30:27
   Jeremiah 23:29

5. How does God confirm the law given on Mt. Sinai in Exodus 19:16-19?

6. What are the similarities to Exodus 19 in the above question and the coming of the Holy Spirit in Acts 2:2-4?

   On Mt. Sinai, God confirmed the validity of the Old Testament law with fire from heaven. At Pentecost, God confirmed the validity of the Holy Spirit's ministry by sending fire. On Mt. Sinai, the fire of God's presence was in one place. At Pentecost, the fire came down on many believers, symbolizing that God's presence is now available to all who believe in him.[66]

7. After Pentecost, how is the Holy Spirit received?
   Acts 8:14-20
   Acts 9:17-19
   Acts 19:5-6

8. How does this compare with the sacrament of confirmation today?

9. What does Jesus say about the role of the Holy Spirit?
   John 15:26-27, Sunday's gospel
   John 16:12-13, Sunday's gospel

10. How will the Holy Spirit glorify Jesus according to Sunday's gospel, John 16:14-15?

11. What are the two different responses to the coming of the Holy Spirit from those gathered in Acts 2:5-7?

Reflection

1. The power of the Holy Spirit came to the disciples in a way that was totally unexpected. Can you think of a time God answered a prayer or worked in a way that you did not expect?

2. Jesus told the disciples about the Holy Spirit. Now they experience the Holy Spirit. What difference does knowledge versus the experience make for them? What is the difference between having knowledge about and experiencing the power of the Holy Spirit for you? How have you experienced the Holy Spirit?

3. One group is "amazed" and asked "what does this mean?" The other group sneers and has a pat answer. Which group do you think you would have been in? In what ways is an attitude of amazement and asking questions a tool for growth?

Optional Exercise. Have each person in the group briefly share about an event from his or her past week or about an upcoming event. This could be a time to share a triumph, trial, or need.

Second Reading

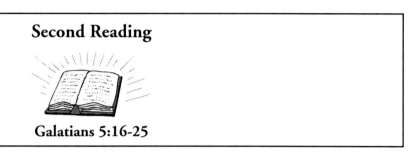

Galatians 5:16-25

Setting the Stage
The second reading is from the letter St. Paul writes about 25 years after the resurrection of Jesus to the Christians living in Galatia (modern-day central Turkey). They are wondering if they need to follow the ancient Jewish Law. St. Paul says that for Christians there is no longer an external law dictating behaviour.[67] Instead, there is an interior source of direction. Through these words of Paul, God our Father names this power He has given us, and He describes its good results, comparing it with the works of "the flesh;" that is, self-centered passions and desires.[68]

Read the second reading. Reread this Scripture. What word, phrase, or idea stands out for you?

Exploring Further

1. How is the law of the Spirit summed up in Galatians 5:14?

2. When we are guided by the Spirit, what two forces begin to battle within us according to Galatians 5:16-17?

3. What are the works of the flesh according to Galatians 5:19-21?

4. How does Paul describe the battle in Romans 7:15, 19-25?

5. What is the fruit or by-product of a life joined with Christ according to Galatians 5:22-23?

6. When self-indulgence rises up in us, what is the remedy?
   Galatians 5:24-25
   Romans 6:6

   Note: At the mystical level of union with the glorified Christ, participation in his death and resurrection through baptism is instantaneous and total, but at the practical level of life on earth, this union has to be grown into gradually. Already "dead" in theory, the Christian must still put this death into practice by "killing" day after day the old, sinful self which still lives in him.[69]

Reflection

1. When hatred, jealousy, rage, envy, selfish ambition, etc., rise up in you, do you believe you are at the mercy of these passions or do you have a choice in how you react? Explain?

2. Practically speaking, how do we crucify our self-indulgent passions?

3. At the Keys of Transformation workshop, by Elijah House Canada, the following format was given for dealing with the ungodly desires that rise up in us.

   a. Name specifically what you are feeling (i.e., revenge, hatred, fear, etc.).
   b. Surrender the desire or feeling to Jesus. (i.e., "Jesus, I choose to give You my desire for revenge," or, "I choose to give You my hatred or hurt feelings," etc. Repent when necessary.
   c. Ask God to replace what you are feeling with something from Him. This may come in the form of a Scripture verse, a song, a sense of peace, or an ability to forgive, etc.

   • When we have been undisciplined or wounded, to choose to turn to God and rely on His power takes practice. Often with intense passions, this needs to be repeated numerous times, maybe even in a single day. As we persevere, the fruit of the Spirit will blossom.
   • Is this tool something that would be useful to you? Why or why not? Divide into pairs and practice this format using a recent incidence from your life.

Closing Prayer

Lord, continue to transform us that we may walk as children of light. Amen.

Trinity Sunday
Year B

Opening Song

Opening Prayer

Open in prayer and invite everyone to add his or her own prayer. Close together: Most Holy Trinity, Creator, Redeemer, and Advocate, we praise and thank You for the love You have shown us. Amen.

Review Study Guidelines

First Reading

Deuteronomy 4:32-34, 39-40

Setting the Stage

The first reading is from the book of Deuteronomy which portrays Moses speaking to the Hebrew people just before they are to enter the Promised Land of Palestine in 1300 B.C. This reading is a magnificent homily about God our Father's decision to "choose the Jews." Two events are underlined. First, He gives them the Ten Commandments on Mount Sinai in the midst of fiery and frightening lightning. Second, He leads them to freedom from slavery in Egypt. What kind of response are should they give? And how should we respond when God calls us out of the bondage of sin?

Read the first reading. Reread this Scripture. What word, phrase, or idea stands out for you?

Exploring Further

1. What great deeds has God done for Israel according to Deuteronomy 4:32-34?

2. When did God speak out of the fire according to Exodus 3:1-6?

3. How does God deliver the Israelites with outstretched arm in Exodus 14:21-28?

4. What is the appropriate response to the wonders God worked in Deuteronomy 4:39?

5. What are we commanded to do and why in Deuteronomy 4:40?

6. What authority does Jesus have according to Sunday's gospel, Matthew 28:16-18?

7. What command are the disciples given and what promise is attached in Sunday's gospel, Matthew 28:19-20?

Reflection

1. God used a burning bush to call Moses. What has God used to call you?

2. The Israelites came to know God through trials, signs, wonders, war, a mighty hand, and terrifying displays of power. What have you come to know about God due to the trials and circumstances in your life?

3. What has convinced you of God's love for you? What has convinced you that God has chosen you and has a purpose and assignment for you? What do you suppose God wants from you and why does God desire you?

4. How can you participate in Jesus' command to baptize, make disciples, and teach? How can you respond to God's call and say yes to Him today?

Optional Exercise. Have each person in the group briefly share about an event from his or her past week or about an upcoming event. This could be a time to share a triumph, trial, or need.

Second Reading

Romans 8:14-17

Setting the Stage

The second reading is from the letter of St. Paul to the church in Rome. It is important to remember that for St. Paul, the name "God" always refers to God the Father. This reading is specifically chosen for Trinity Sunday because we see how all three Persons of the Blessed Trinity are at work in our lives. Note also that "Abba" is the Aramaic word meaning something more like "Daddy" or "Papa" rather than the more formal word, "Father."

Read the second reading aloud. Reread this Scripture. What word, phrase, or idea stands out for you?

Exploring Further

1. What is the result of being led by the Spirit in Romans 8:14?

2. What does the Spirit give?
   Romans 8:15-16
   Romans 5:5

3. In what intimate way are we able to address God according to Romans 8:15b?

4. In what circumstances did Jesus pray calling God "Abba" in Mark 14:32-36?

5. What do we learn regarding God and love in 1 John 4:10, 15-19?

6. How is God's love depicted in Hosea 11:3-4?

7. As children of God, what is now our "legal" status according to Romans 8:17a?

8. What promise did God make to Abraham in Genesis 22:17-18?

9. How is this promise fulfilled, as explained in Galatians 3:26-29?

10. What two aspects are involved with being joint heirs with Christ in Romans 8:17b?

11. What reward follows sharing in Christ's' sufferings?
    Mark 10:28-30
    Luke 22:28-30

Reflection

1. How can we be led by the Spirit? How can we know we are being led by the Spirit?

2. Can you think of a time when you cried out to God from the depths of your being? What was the result? How would you describe your relationship with God the Father?

3. Have you ever received an inheritance? What effect did it have on you? Are you in line to receive an inheritance? What does it mean to you?

4. What does being God's heir and joint heir with Christ mean to you? What, in your eternal inheritance, are you looking forward to? How are we already sharing in this inheritance?

5. What suffering may be involved if we are to remain faithful to Jesus? How can comfort and complacency be a danger to faithfulness?

Closing Prayer

Thank You for pouring Your Holy Spirit into our hearts, allowing us to cry out, "Abba, Father." Your steadfast love is upon us. Our hope is in You. Amen.

BODY AND BLOOD OF CHRIST
YEAR B

Opening Song

Opening Prayer

Open in prayer and invite everyone to add his or her own prayer. Close together: I will take the cup of salvation and call on the name of the Lord. Amen.

Review Study Guidelines

First Reading

Exodus 24:3-8

Setting the Stage

The first reading is from the book of Exodus, which tells the story of the escape of the Hebrew people from slavery in Egypt under the leadership of Moses in 1300 B.C. On their way, they receive from God our Father the Ten Commandments, and we hear today how they respond. In the readings we hear about the religious custom of slaughtering animals and using their blood for worship. To kill oxen, calves, lambs, goats, and other living creatures is a sign of giving one's life totally to God. It is done in different ways:

1. Sometimes the animal is killed and cooked, and then the meat eaten as a sign of union with God.
2. Sometimes the animal is killed and completely burned up; this is called a burnt offering and is a sign of adoration.

Note that the blood of the animal is first drained off, then used in ritual; it is a symbol of life. Today's reading shows Moses sprinkling first the altar and then the people with the blood, symbolizing the union between God and His people. They give their life to Him and He gives His life to them. This action formed a "covenant"—a bonding, a close relationship between them.

Read the first reading aloud. Reread this Scripture. What word, phrase, or idea stands out for you?

Exploring Further

1. After Moses reads the words of the Lord—the Decalogue or Ten Commandments—what is the response of the people in Exodus 24:3?

2. On a number of occasions the Israelites promise to serve God. What reasons do the people give for serving God in Joshua 24:16-18?

3. Why is the decision to serve God not entered into lightly according to Joshua 24:19-24?

4. What is Moses' role?
   Exodus 24:2
   Deuteronomy 5:26-27

5. How does Moses prepare for the time of sacrifice in Exodus 24:4-5?

6. How does Jesus have preparations made ready in Sunday's gospel Mark 14:12-16?

7. What is the ritual Moses uses to ratify the covenant, uniting God and the people in Exodus 24:6-8?

8. How does Jesus, the new mediator, ratify the new covenant?
   Mark 14:22-25, Sunday's gospel
   Hebrews 9:12-22

Reflection

1. When Moses proclaims the Word of God, the people respond, "We will obey." When have you heard or read God's Word and the words seemed alive or as if they were speaking right to you? What response rose up in you? What have you discovered while trying to be faithful and obedient to your promises?

2. How do you ritualize important decisions or occasions in your life, both at church and at home?

3. What is the importance of blood, both physically and spiritually, to life, health, family, faith, etc.

Optional Exercise. Have each person in the group briefly share about an event from his or her past week or about an upcoming event. This could be a time to share a triumph, trial, or need.

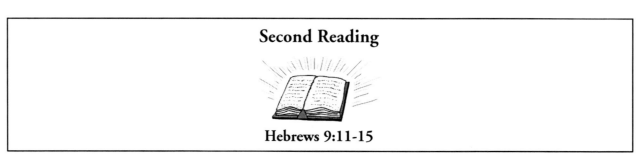

Second Reading

Hebrews 9:11-15

Setting the Stage

The second reading is from the letter to the Hebrews. The writer is a Jew who has become a Christian and is encouraging other Jewish Christians to keep the faith by drawing on their Jewish history. This reading is full of comparisons:

1. The writer shows the differences between what Jesus does and what the Jewish high priest does.
2. He also makes the Jewish temple in Jerusalem a symbol of heaven, which is the new "Tent" and new "Holy Place."[70]
3. The old covenant, which is the first pact, made in the blood of animals and described in our first reading today, is compared to how the new covenant, the new relationship, between God our Father and us, comes to be. We hear what is given to us because of what Jesus did.

Read the second reading. Reread this Scripture. What word, phrase, or idea stands out for you?

Exploring Further

1. What does Christ come as according to Hebrews 9:11?

2. What does the high priest do once a year and for what purpose in Hebrews 9:6-7?

3. What tent or sanctuary or "holy of holies" does Jesus enter in Hebrews 9:24?

4. According to the law, what does shedding of blood do in Hebrews 9:22?

5. What type of animal has to be used for sacrifice according to Numbers 19:2?

6. What is the offering Jesus used for the sacrifice?
    Hebrews 9:12
    1 Peter 1:18-19

7. What is the effect of this sacrifice for us?
    Hebrews 9:12b-14
    Hebrews 10:19-22
    Romans 3:23-24

Reflection

1. There are several songs that use the phrase "power in the blood." How would you explain to someone the results of Jesus' shed blood for us?

2. In Romans and Ephesians the sacrifice of Jesus is described as a gift. Can this gift be earned or deserved? Why or why not? Can this gift be accepted or rejected? Why or why not?

3. Consider the following reflection.[71]

    A decision joins us to the eternal. It brings what is eternal into time. A decision raises us with a shock from the slumber of monotony. A decision pronounces a blessing upon even the weakest beginning, as long as it is a real beginning. Decision is the awakening to the eternal...a road well begun is the battle half won. The important thing is to make a beginning and get under way. There is nothing more harmful for your soul than to hold back and not get moving.

The archenemy of decision is cowardice. Cowardice is constantly at work trying to break off the good agreement of decision with eternity...Cowardice hides behind the thought it likes best—the crutch of time. Cowardice and time always find a reason for not hurrying, saying "Not today, but tomorrow," whereas God in heaven and the eternal say: "Do it today. Now is the day of salvation." The eternal refrain of decision is: "Today, today."

- What decisions have you made regarding your faith and the free gift of redemption that Jesus offers? Are there any decisions you are putting off for another day?

4. In what way do fear and procrastination hold you back on your faith journey?

5. How does "waiting on the Lord" and not making a decision differ?

Closing Prayer

Thank You for redeeming us with the precious blood of the Lamb, Your Son, Jesus Christ. Help us to understand in a deeper way what this gift of redemption means, causing us to respond with ever deepening gratitude and love. Amen.

Appendix One
Deuterocanonical Books/Apocrypha

The following books are considered the Deuterocanonical or Apocrypha: Tobit, Judith, Sirach (Ecclesiasticus), Wisdom, 1 & 2 Maccabees, Baruch, and parts of Daniel.

Among Christians it was apparently not until the fourth century that the issue of canonicity (to recognize officially inspired books to be included in the Bible) of these books arose.

In 1546, at the Council of Trent, the Roman Catholic Church officially declared these books to be sacred and canonical and to be accepted "with equal devotion and reverence."

At the time of the Reformation, Martin Luther did not regard these books as Scripture, but as *useful and good for reading.* In his German translation of the Bible, he placed them at the end of the Old Testament with the superscription "Apocrypha." Protestants generally continued this practice in their translations of the Bible.

Catholics speak of these books as "Deuterocanonical" to indicate that their canonical status as Scripture was settled later than that of the "Protocanonical" books. Others usually refer to these books as the Apocrypha.[72]

For this Bible study I suggest you bring a Bible that includes the Apocrypha as there are some readings from this section each year. If you have a Catholic Bible, these books will automatically be included. If you have a Protestant Bible, the Apocrypha will not be included unless stated "with Apocrypha."

APPENDIX TWO
DEFINITION OF "WORLD" AS USED IN SCRIPTURE

The word "world" is used in three ways in Scripture:

1. *World* can refer to the physical creation. It is used in this way in Genesis.[73]

2. *World* can refer to all that is hostile to God—all that stands in enmity with God. Love of the world reflects attachment to what is transitory. Love of God brings Christians into relationship with what "remains" forever.[74] It is used this way in 1, 2, and 3 John.

3. *World* can refer to people in general. It is used this way in John 3:16, "For God so loved the world that he sent his only Son, so that every one who believes in him may not perish but may have eternal life."

Appendix Three
Epistles and Letters of the New Testament

These ditties or rhythms may be used as an aid to remember the order of books in the New Testament.

Matthew	Matthew, Mark, Luke,
Mark	and John,
Luke	hold the horse while
John	I get on
Acts	Acting
Romans	Romans
1 Corinthians	Carry
2 Corinthians	Crosses
Galatians	Go
Ephesians	Eat
Philippians	Pop
Colossians	Corn
1 Thessalonians	Teasing
2 Thessalonians	Tess
1 Timothy	Tries
2 Timothy	Tim's
Titus	Temper
Philemon	Please
Hebrews	Help
James	James
1 Peter	Prepare
2 Peter	Peter
1 John	
2 John	
3 John	3 Johns
Jude	Joyfully
Revelation	Repent

ENDNOTES
ALL NOTES ARE USED WITH PERMISSION

1. *The Word Among Us*, September 2003 (9639 Dr. Perry Road, Suite 126, Ijamsville, Maryland, 21754: The Word Among Us Press, www.wordamongus.org.), p. 34. Used with permission.

2. *New Jerome Biblical Commentary* (New Jersey: Prentice Hall, 1990), p. 330, 3&4.

3. *New Jerome Biblical Commentary* (New Jersey: Prentice Hall, 1990), p. 791.

4. Annotated Bible with Apocrypha, NRSV (New York: Oxford University Press, 1991), Philippians 1:15-18 note.

5. *Secrets of the Vine* (2001), B. Wilkinson (Sisters: Multnomah Publishing Incorporate, 2001), p. 35, 58, 62, 96, 110. Used with permission.

6. *Fanning into Flame the Gifts You Received*, Ryan, Ron (Western Washington: Catholic Charismatic Renewal. © 1992) audiotape series.

7. The New Jerusalem Bible (Garden City, New York: Doubleday & Company, Inc., 1985), 1 Thess. 1, note c.

8. The New Jerusalem Bible (Garden City, New York: Doubleday & Company, Inc., 1985), Acts 3, note n.

9. The New Jerusalem Bible (Garden City, New York: Doubleday & Company, Inc., 1985), 1Thess. 2, note d.

10. *Catechism of the Catholic Church* (Ottawa: Publication Service, Canadian Conference of Catholic Bishops, 1994), n 134.

11. *Our Daily Bread* (Windsor: RBC Ministries), Oct 29, 1999.

12. The New Jerusalem Bible (Garden City, New York: Doubleday & Company, Inc., 1985), Matt. 5, note a.

13. *Catechism of the Catholic Church* (Ottawa: Publication Service, Canadian Conference of Catholic Bishops, 1994), n 1030.

14. The New American Bible (New York: Catholic Book Publishing Company, 1992), note Lam. 3:27.

15. N. Gumbel, *Questions of Life* (Colorado: Cook Communications Ministries, 1993, 1996), p.129. Used with permission of Kingsway Publishing and Cook Communications Ministries.

16. Jerome Biblical Commentary (New Jersey: Prentice Hall, 1968), p. 384, no. 63.

17. Life Application Bible, New Revised Standard Version (Wheaton, Illinois: Tyndale House Publishers, 1990), note Is. 40:11.

18. Jerome Biblical Commentary (New Jersey: Prentice Hall, 1968), p. 233.

19. *Radical Grace*, R. Rohr (Cincinnati: St. Anthony Messenger Press, 1995), p. 324.

20. Annotated Bible with Apocrypha, NRSV (New York: Oxford University Press, 1991), note 2 Sam. 7.

21. *Life Application Bible*, New Revised Standard Version (Wheaton, Illinois: Tyndale House Publishers, 1990), note Luke 1:36-37.

22. *Life Application Bible*, New Revised Standard Version (Wheaton, Illinois: Tyndale House Publishers, 1990), note 7.2.

23. The New Jerusalem Bible (Garden City, New York: Doubleday & Company, Inc., 1985), Jn. 4 note a.

24. The New Jerusalem Bible (Garden City, New York: Doubleday & Company, Inc., 1985), Jn. 19 note r.

25. *St. Joseph Edition* of The New American Bible (New York: Catholic Book Publishing Company, 1986), note 1Jn. 5:6-12.

26. *Catechism of the Catholic Church* (Ottawa: Publication Service, Canadian Conference of Catholic Bishops, 1994), n. 1170.

27. *The Good News about Sex and Marriage Seminar, course workbook*, C. West (Denver: Existence Studios, 2002), p.13.

28. *Catechism of the Catholic Church* (Ottawa: Publication Service, Canadian Conference of Catholic Bishops, 1994), n. 1607.

29. The New Jerusalem Bible (Garden City, New York: Doubleday & Company, Inc., 1985), Gn. 6 note d.

30. The New American Bible (New York: Catholic Book Publishing Company, 1992), note 1 Cor. 7:29-31.

31. *The Good News about Sex and Marriage Seminar*, course workbook, Christopher West (Denver, Co: Existence Studios, 2002), p. 25, 26.

32. *Good News about Sex & Marriage*, Christopher West (Ann Arbor, MI: Servant Publication, 2000), p. 160-161.

33. The New American Bible (New York: Catholic Book Publishing Company, 1992), footnote Nbs. 12:10.

34. The New Jerusalem Bible (Garden City, New York: Doubleday & Company, Inc., 1985), Ex. 13 note d.

35. The New Jerusalem Bible (Garden City, New York: Doubleday & Company, Inc., 1985), Hos. 2 note p.

36. *Life Application Bible*, New Revised Standard Version (Wheaton, Illinois: Tyndale House Publishers, 1990), note Mark 2:22.

37. Annotated Bible with Apocrypha, NRSV (New York: Oxford University Press, 1991), page 217.

38. Ex 20:8, note f.

39. *Catechism of the Catholic Church* (Ottawa: Publication Service, Canadian Conference of Catholic Bishops, 1994), n.2176.

40. Annotated Bible with Apocrypha, NRSV (New York: Oxford University Press, 1991), note 2 Cor. 4:4.

41. The New Jerusalem Bible (Garden City, New York: Doubleday & Company, Inc., 1985), Jn. 8, note b.

42. *Catechism of the Catholic Church* (Ottawa: Publication Service, Canadian Conference of Catholic Bishops, 1994), n. 1521.

43. *A Father Who Keeps his Promises* Scott Hahn (Ann Arbor, MI: Servant Publication, 1998), parts of p. 23, 28.

44. *A Father Who Keeps his Promises* Scott Hahn (Ann Arbor, MI: Servant Publication, 1998), parts of p.35.

45. *A Father Who Keeps his Promises* Scott Hahn (Ann Arbor, MI: Servant Publication, 1998), parts of p.36.

46. *Catechism of the Catholic Church* (Ottawa: Publication Service, Canadian Conference of Catholic Bishops, 1994), n. 632.

47. *Catechism of the Catholic Church* (Ottawa: Publication Service, Canadian Conference of Catholic Bishops, 1994), n. 634.

48. *The Great Themes of Scripture*, R. Rohr and J. Martos (Cincinnati: St. Anthony Messenger Press, 1987), p.30.

49. *Radical Grace*, R. Rohr (Cincinnati: St. Anthony Messenger Press, 1995), p. 14.

50. The New Jerusalem Bible (Garden City, New York: Doubleday & Company, Inc., 1985), 1 Cor. 1, note r.

51. Reprinted from *The Word Among Us*, Lent Edition 1996, The Word Among Us Press (9639 Dr. Perry Road, Suite 126, Ijamsville, Maryland, 21754, www.wordamongus.org.), Used with permission.

52. The New Jerusalem Bible (Garden City, New York: Doubleday & Company, Inc., 1985), Jer. 31, note l.

53. *Life Application Bible*, New Revised Standard Version (Wheaton, Illinois: Tyndale House Publishers, 1990), note Hebrews, 5:9.

54. The New Jerusalem Bible (Garden City, New York: Doubleday & Company, Inc., 1985), Supplements, Chronological table.

55. *Life Application Bible*, New Revised Standard Version (Wheaton, Illinois: Tyndale House Publishers, 1990), note Acts 10:34.

56. The New Jerusalem Bible (Garden City, New York: Doubleday & Company, Inc., 1985), Mt. 8:29, note k.

57. The New Jerusalem Bible (Garden City, New York: Doubleday & Company, Inc., 1985), Introduction to John.

58. New Jerome Biblical Commentary (New Jersey, Prentice Hall, 1990), 82:44.

59. New Jerome Biblical Commentary (New Jersey, Prentice Hall 1990), 47:32 and 62:2.

60. The New Jerusalem Bible (Garden City, New York: Doubleday & Company, Inc., 1985), 1 John 2:3 note a.

61. *Life Application Bible*, New Revised Standard Version (Wheaton, Illinois: Tyndale House Publishers, 1990), Acts 4, note 4:1, ... 4:2, 3.

62. The New Jerusalem Bible (Garden City, New York: Doubleday & Company, Inc., 1985), Acts 3:16, note l.

63. Reprinted from *The Word Among Us*, Easter Edition 2003, The Word Among Us Press (9639 Dr. Perry Road, Suite 126, Ijamsville, Maryland, 21754, www.wordamongus.org.), Used with permission

64. The New Jerusalem Bible (Garden City, New York: Doubleday & Company, Inc., 1985), note Acts 4a.

65. Bishop Henry - Western Catholic Reporter, June 12, 2000 edition, page three.

66. *Life Application Bible*, New Revised Standard Version (Wheaton, Illinois: Tyndale House Publishers, 1990), Acts 4, note Acts 2:3, 4.

67. The New Jerusalem Bible (Garden City, New York: Doubleday & Company, Inc., 1985), note Gal. 5:23, note 1.

68. Jerome Biblical Commentary (New Jersey: Prentice Hall, 1968), no. 30 and Annotated Bible with Apocrypha, NRSV (New York: Oxford University Press, 1991), Rom. 7:15; Rom. 8:5.

69. The New Jerusalem Bible (Garden City, New York: Doubleday & Company, Inc., 1985), note Col. 3c.

70. The New Jerusalem Bible (Garden City, New York: Doubleday & Company, Inc., 1985), Heb. 9:12, note g.

71. *Living Faith Daily Catholic Devotions*, S. Kierkgaard (Ottawa, Novalis, Saint Paul University, 2000), Vol. 16, Number 2, Tues., July 18, 2000.

72. Good News Bible (American Bible Society, 1979), Introduction to the Deuterocanonical/Apocryphal Books.

73. New Jerome Biblical Commentary (New Jersey, Prentice Hall, 1990), 82:44.

74. New Jerome Biblical Commentary (New Jersey, Prentice Hall 1990), 47:32; 62:21.

Printed in the United States
123701LV00006B/3-16/P

9 781414 111599